Victoria Road characters

Tom Hutchinson

hotline

pre-intermediate

student's book

OXFORD UNIVERSITY PRESS 1992

contents

Terry and Sue

1 **Look at the people on the front page. Do you know their names?**

a Look quickly through the story and check their names.

b One of the characters is not mentioned. Which one? Look through the book. When will you meet her in this book?

c What do you know about the characters?

2 **Look at this episode. What are the people doing?**

3 **Listen and follow in your books.**

Terry Hi, Casey.

Casey Hello, Terry. How's your new job? Are you enjoying it?

Terry Yes, it's great.

Casey What do you do?

Terry I work for a London newspaper. How's school these days? Are you in the same class as Vince and Sue?

Casey Not really. We do different subjects. Vince does Physics, Maths and Chemistry. Sue does Computer Studies, History and Geography, I think. And I do English, French and History. So we don't see each other very often.

Terry Have you seen Kamala lately? I haven't seen her since she went to college.

Casey I saw her on Monday at the leisure centre. She was playing badminton with Sue. I didn't recognize her at first. She looked very different.

Terry Hey. Guess what. I had a letter from Jackie yesterday. She's still in America. I don't think she'll come back to England.

Casey Well, she won't come back to Victoria Road. Her parents have moved.

Casey Look. Isn't that Mr Scott's car?

Terry Yes, but he wasn't driving. It was Sue.

Casey Is she learning to drive?

Terry Yes, she and Vince are both learning. Look she's stopping.

Sue Is it still OK for our date tomorrow night, Terry?

Terry Oh, er, no. I forgot. I've got to work late tomorrow. I'm sorry.

Sue Terry, you're impossible. Well, I'll see you at the weekend, then.

Terry OK. See you at the weekend. Stand back, Casey.

Sue Oh, ha, ha. Very funny!

4 **Complete these sentences with the correct names.**

a .... have left school.

b .... works for a newspaper.

c .... goes to college.

d .... are still at school.

e .... studies Science subjects.

f .... studies a foreign language.

g .... study History.

h .... lives in America.

i .... have left Victoria Road.

j .... looks different.

k .... are learning to drive.

l .... are going out together.

5 **Close your book. Listen to the dialogue again.**

Useful expressions

6 **How do you say these in your language?**

What do you do? ¿Qué haces?

these days Estos días

We don't see each other.

Nosotros no nos vemos.

Have you seen ... lately?

Le has visto últimamente.

I didn't recognize her at first.

Guess what. Adivínalo

She's learning to drive.

Está aprendiendo a conducir.

Is it still OK for our date?

Tenemos hoy la cita?

I've got to work late.

Tengo que llegar tarde.

You're impossible. Eres imposible.

Stand back. ~~[illegible]~~ Quítate.

Very funny! ~~Muy~~ Gracioso

7 **Work in groups of three. Each person takes one of the parts. Read the dialogue.**

FOLLOW UP

8 **Answer these questions.**

a Where does Terry work?
b What subjects does Sue study?
c What does Kamala do?
d Where did Casey see Kamala?
e What was she doing?
f Why didn't he recognize her?
g Why won't Jackie come back to Victoria Road?
h Whose car did Terry and Casey see?
i Why wasn't Mr Scott driving?
j What has Terry forgotten?

LANGUAGE WORK

Tense revision

1 **Do you recognize the tenses you have learnt?**

a Put the verbs in these sentences into the table.

I work for a London newspaper.
She's stopping.
She won't come back here.
She was playing badminton.
Have you seen Kamala lately?
I saw her at the leisure centre.

tense	
future	I'll work for a London
present simple	~~I~~ Work for a London newspaper
present continuous	She's stopping
present perfect	Have you seen Kamala lately
past simple	I saw her at the leisure centre
past continuous	She was playing badminton.

b Find more examples of each tense in the Victoria Road story.

2 **Here is Terry's letter to Jackie. Write the verbs in brackets in the correct tense.**

20 Victoria Road
Hartfield
Bucks
HA6 4BJ

2nd October

Dear Jackie,

Thank you very much for your letter. It was great to hear from you.

I have left school. I ______ (leave) in July. I ______ (be) fed up with it and I ______ (want) to earn some money. I ______ (work) for a newspaper in London. It's great.

Kamala ______ (leave) school, too. She ______ (go) to college now. I ______ (not see) her since she ______ (go) to college. Casey ______ (see) her last week. She ______ (play) badminton with Sue. Casey says he ______ (not recognize) her, because she ______ (look) very different.

Vince, Sue and Casey ______ (be) still at school, but they all ______ (study) different subjects. So they ______ (not see) each other very often. I ______ (go out) with Sue now.

Sue and Vince ______ (learn) to drive. They ______ (be) 17 last month. Mr Scott ______ (teach) them in his car. I ______ (see) them yesterday. Sue ______ (drive). I'll be 17 in three months time. Then I ______ (learn) to drive.

______ you ______ (stay) in the States? Your parents ______ (move) in the summer, so I suppose you ______ (not come) back here. Some new people ______ (move) into your old house, but I ______ (not meet) them yet.

Well that's all the news for now. I hope that you ______ (write) again. Bye for now,

love,

Terry

P.S. We took this photo at our school leaving picnic.

FOLLOW UP

3 **Look at Terry's letter. Find the answers to these questions. Write the answers in complete sentences.**

a When did Terry leave school?
b Why did he leave?
c When can you learn to drive a car in Britain?
d When is Vince's birthday?
e When is Terry's birthday?

PROJECT

Your life

1 Work in groups. Imagine one of your classmates left your school a year ago. Write a letter to him/her with all the news from your group.

a Discuss what you will write about. You can write about:

- changes in each person's life: new hobbies, learning to drive;
- changes at school: a new teacher, new people in the class, new subjects;
- changes in the area: new roads, new buildings;
- important things in the past year: holidays, visitors;
- any gossip or 'scandal'.

b Write your letter. Use Terry's letter as a model.

c Show your letter to other groups.

2 Write an extra paragraph for the letter about changes in your family. You can write about:

- marriages, births, new house, new jobs etc.

My parents gave me a hi-fi for my birthday. It's fantastic.

There's a new cafe in town called 'Hot Spot'. We often meet up there for a drink.

Tim and Jenny are going out together now.

This summer we went camping at the seaside.

I'm learning to drive. It's great fun but I was a bit nervous at first.

▶ **Pronunciation: page 112**

1 lifestyles

present tenses: revision

Contents

Learning objectives

In this unit you will revise the present tenses in order to:

- describe regular activities and events
- describe lifestyles

You will also learn a new use of the present continuous tense to:

- make arrangements
- describe future plans

Preview task

What can you remember?

- What are the two present tenses? Find an example of each one in this unit.
- What is the difference between them?
- Write down two things that you know about each tense.

Carol's keys

1 What do you remember? What happened in the last part of the story? Look back at page 4 and check your ideas.

2 Look at this episode. Who are the people? Where are they? What are they doing?

3 Listen and follow in your books.

Last Wednesday at the station

Terry Where's Carol this morning? Isn't she going to work today?

Friend Oh, she's always late. Look, there she is. She's parking the car now. Come on, Carol, the train's coming. She won't make it.

On the train

Terry You just made it.

Carol Wait a minute. My keys. Stop the train. I've left my keys in the car!

On Saturday

Terry Carol travels to work by train with me, but she goes to the station every day by car and she parks the car at the station. It's a really smart sports car. The train leaves at twenty-five past eight. Carol's always late and she rushes for the train. Well, last Wednesday, it was so funny . . .

Behind a tree

Kamala What are you doing, Casey?

Casey I'm hiding from Terry. He's telling that story about Carol's keys again.

Kamala Oh no! He tells that story all the time. He's becoming a real bore. He only talks about the people at the office these days.

Casey Yes, he doesn't really belong to our group any more. Oh, I'm sorry, Sue. I didn't mean . . . . Well, I know you're going out with him, but . . .

Sue Oh it's all right. I know what you mean.

Kamala Look out. He's coming. He'll see us.

Terry Hello, you lot. Why are you hiding behind that tree?

Casey We aren't hiding. We . . . er . . . we're . . . er . . . we're looking for . . . er . . .

Kamala . . . for Sue's keyring.

Sue Oh no! Don't mention keys.

Terry That reminds me. Have I told you the story about Carol and her keys?

Casey Oh, er, I must be off. Bye.

Kamala Me, too. See you Terry.

Terry Hey. What about Sue's keyring?

Sue Shall I tell him?

What do you think?

- What has happened to Terry?
- What will Sue do?

4 Right, Wrong or Don't know?

	✓	✖	?
a Carol and Terry work in the same office.	☐	☐	☐
b Carol travels to work by car every day.	☐	☐	☐
c Last Wednesday Carol missed the train.	☐	☐	☐
d Someone stole Carol's car, because she left the keys in it.	☐	☐	☐
e Terry has told the story about Carol before.	☐	☐	☐
f Casey doesn't want to talk to Terry.	☐	☐	☐
g Kamala thinks Terry is a bore.	☐	☐	☐
h Kamala is going out with Terry.	☐	☐	☐
i Casey, Kamala and Sue are looking for a keyring.	☐	☐	☐

5 Close your book. Listen to the dialogue again.

Useful expressions

6 **How do you say these in your language?**

There she is.	ahí está ella
She won't make it.	Casi lo pierdes
You just made it.	Lo cogió por poco.
a really smart sports car	Es un deportivo elegantísimo
a real bore	un aburrimiento
You're going out with him.	Tu estás saliendo con él
I know what you mean.	Sé lo que quieres decir
Hello, you lot.	Hola a todos.
Don't mention ...	No lo digas.
That reminds me.	ahora que me recuerdas de algo
I must be off.	Debo irme
Me, too.	Yo también.

7 **Work in groups of four. One person is Terry, one person is Kamala, another person is Sue and Carol, and the other person is Casey and the friend. Read the dialogue.**

FOLLOW UP

8 **Complete the passage.**

Terry I'll help you look for your ....Keyring...., Sue.

Sue It's all ....right...., Terry. They weren't looking ....for.... my keyring.

Terry What were they ....?

Sue They were .... from you.

Terry Why?

Sue .... were telling that story about .... keys again. You ....tells.... that story every ....day.... anyone sees you. You're .... a real .... You only .... about the people at the .... these days. You .... really belong .... our group ....

Terry Oh. I see.

LANGUAGE WORK

Present tenses: revision

1 **Read the Victoria Road story again. Pay particular attention to the tenses.**

a Complete these sentences with the correct form of the verb.

----------	----------
She .... the car at the station every day.	She's .... the car now.
He .... that story all the time.	He.................. that story about Carol's keys again.
....	....

b What are the two tenses called? Write their names above the correct column.

c Find more examples of each in the Victoria Road story. Add them to the correct column.

d What is the difference in meaning between the two tenses? The words below will help you.

every day   all the time   now   again

Terry's day

2 **Look at the pictures opposite.**

a What is Terry doing in each picture?

b Describe Terry's day.

c How would Terry describe his day?

d What do you think about Terry's new lifestyle? Does it look exciting or boring?

Future simple: revision

3 **Look at the Victoria Road story on page 10.**

a Complete these sentences.

She ..won't.......... make it.
He.'ll............ see us.

b Arrange these words in the table below to show the future simple.

will	He	You	'll
It	I	won't	We
She	will not	They	

I	....	work in an office.
You	....	go to college.
He	....	travel to work by train.
She	....	
It		
We		
They		

4 **How do you think your life will change when you leave school? Write down five things that you will do and five things that you won't do.**

FOLLOW UP

5 **Write your answers for a and b in Exercise 2.**

WORDSQUARE

In this wordsquare there are six days of the week and eleven months. Find the missing day and month.

D	G	O	F	N	A	U	G	U	P	R	O	M	U	M	N
W	E	D	N	E	S	D	A	Y	U	D	V	G	C	A	O
O	N	L	Y	S	U	N	P	T	M	F	E	B	R	Y	V
B	B	L	F	L	N	S	E	P	T	E	M	B	E	R	E
R	U	G	A	P	D	V	Z	E	F	W	B	U	H	T	L
J	C	R	U	D	A	P	R	I	L	R	T	S	R	S	T
E	N	O	G	Q	Y	J	M	R	E	S	O	E	P	A	M
D	S	J	U	K	X	R	U	B	D	A	B	P	A	Y	O
N	O	V	E	M	B	E	R	N	V	M	E	T	A	B	N
F	R	I	D	A	Y	T	C	E	E	W	T	D	R	U	D
M	D	N	X	P	T	D	A	C	O	C	R	V	J	K	A
A	O	M	B	S	Y	W	E	I	T	U	E	S	D	A	Y
R	F	E	U	S	U	D	E	M	T	L	M	P	O	K	T
C	L	G	M	A	M	A	J	A	N	U	A	R	Y	R	H
H	U	W	E	T	U	E	S	U	S	T	R	I	L	V	U
A	P	N	S	O	C	T	O	B	E	R	C	L	E	A	R

READING

The Amish

1 Look at the pictures and say what you think.

a Who are the people?

b What are they doing?

c Where do they live?

d Why are they wearing these clothes?

2 Now read the text quickly. Check your ideas.

Imagine a world without telephones or television, without cars or electricity. In this world the women wear long dresses. There is no industry. Everyone works on farms and travels by horse or on foot. Where do you think this world is? Europe in the seventeenth century, perhaps? In fact, it is Pennsylvania in America in the 1990s. It is the world of the Amish people.

The Amish people went to America in the eighteenth century and since then their lifestyle has not changed at all. They don't even speak English among themselves. They speak German as their ancestors did. The Amish are farmers and they base their life on the Bible. There were no tractors or telephones in the Bible and there are no tractors or telephones in the Amish villages today.

Amish life is very strict and very simple. Their clothes are very plain. The men and boys wear dark jackets and trousers, plain shirts and hats. The women and girls wear long dresses and small bonnets. They have long hair and they don't wear any make-up or jewellery.

Family life is very important for the Amish. They live in large families and everyone helps with the work. The day starts when the sun rises and it ends when the sun sets. The men and boys work in the fields and the women and girls work in the house. When something big is needed, such as a new barn, all the neighbours help to build it. While the men and boys cut, lift and hammer the wood, the women and girls prepare the food and look after the children. Nobody works on Sundays, because everyone goes to church.

But life for the Amish is not all work. They have a lot of village parties. They don't dance or play musical instruments, but they sing hymns and they have a good time.

There is no electricity in the world of the Amish. They don't use chemicals on their farms. The rules are strict. But there is no crime and no pollution. Nobody is poor and nobody is lonely.

3 Read the text again. Find out these things about Amish boys and girls.

- things that an Amish girl does but an Amish boy doesn't
- things that an Amish boy does but an Amish girl doesn't
- things that both boys and girls do
- things that neither boys nor girls do

4 Here is part of an interview with an Amish girl. Her answers are below the questions. Write the number of the right answer beside each question.

Where do you live? ...3.....

Where did your ancestors come from? ...8.....

Do you speak English? ...1.....

Have you got any brothers or sisters? ...5.....

When do you get up? ...2.....

What do you do? ...6.....

Does you brother work in the house, too? ...9.....

Why don't you have telephones and cars? ...7.....

Do you like your lifestyle? ...4.....

1 Yes, but at home we speak German.
2 Very early in the morning, when the sun rises.
3 In a village in Pennsylvania.
4 Yes, I do. I like my lifestyle very much.
5 Yes, I've got one brother and two sisters.
6 My sisters and I work in the house. We cook and clean and wash.
7 We base our life on the Bible. People didn't have telephones and cars in the Bible, so we don't have them.
8 They came from Germany.
9 No, he works in the fields with my father.

5 What do you think of the Amish lifestyle?

a Read the text again and organize all the information about the Amish into three lists like this.

What I think are ...		
good things about Amish life	bad things about Amish life	things which are neither good nor bad

b Explain your answers.

WORD WORK

6 Look through the text and underline all the plural nouns. Write the singular of each one.

FOLLOW UP

7 Write a paragraph describing your lifestyle to an Amish boy or girl.

LISTENING

Sue and Terry's date

1 **Listen to the conversation.**

a What are Terry and Sue doing this evening?

b Why is Terry phoning Sue?

c When will they see each other?

d What does Sue say Terry's problem is?

2 **Here are Sue's and Terry's diaries. Listen and write what they are doing this week.**

Present continuous with future meaning

3 **Listen to the conversation again. Pay attention to the tenses.**

a Complete these sentences.

We' .... in half an hour.

I' .... badminton tomorrow night.

.... you .... anything on Thursday?

What' .... on Friday?

Carol' .... a party on Friday.

b What tense is used?

c Look at the words that tell us when the arrangement is for, e.g. tomorrow night. These are called time expressions. Find the time expressions in the sentences above.

d What time are the sentences about?

the past the present the future

e Complete this rule.

> **The present ______________ tense + a future time expression shows a __________ arrangement or event.**

4 **Giving reasons**

Why can't they make it? What reasons do Terry and Sue give?

Terry, Monday: ....

Sue, Tuesday: ....

Terry, Wednesday: ....

Sue, Thursday: ....

Terry, Friday: ....

5 **What do you think of Terry and Sue's argument? Who is right?**

FOLLOW UP

6 **Write the answers to Exercise 4. Start like this:**

On Monday evening Terry can't make it because he . . .

INTERACTION

Making arrangements

1 📼 **Listen to Sue and Terry's conversation again. How do they suggest times for a date? Complete this part of the conversation.**

Terry .... tomorrow night?

Sue That's no good. I'm playing badminton tomorrow night. You know I play badminton every Tuesday.

Terry .... after you've finished?

Sue I don't finish till 9.30. And I usually go to the cafe with Kamala afterwards. ....
.... ?

Terry No, I can't make it on Wednesday. I want to watch the football match on TV. ....
.... ?

2 **Is there anything in your diary for next week?**

a Write an activity for three evenings in the diary below. Put the times next to each one. Don't show your diary to anyone.

b Work in pairs. Each student takes one of the roles, A or B. Use the conversation between Terry and Sue to help you. Remember these expressions.

Are you free on ...?	That's no good.
What about ...?	I can't. I've got to ...
How about ...?	I always ... on
Are you doing anything on ...?	

Act your telephone conversation.

A: You have a date on Monday with **B**. You are going to the cinema. You really want to go, but you can't make it. Telephone **B**, explain why you can't make it and try to arrange another date.

B: You have a date on Monday with **A**, but you don't want to go. You don't really like the boy/girl, but you don't want to hurt his/her feelings. When **A** telephones, try not to make another date.

FOLLOW UP

3 **Use your diary. Write a conversation arranging a date.**

PROJECT

Your lifestyle

1 Who is your lifestyle influenced by?

a Work in groups or pairs. Make a list of all the groups of people that influence your life.

b Discuss these questions.

- How much time do you spend with each group in a week?
- What things do you do with each group?
- What things don't you do with each group?
- Are there any group rules?

2 Draw a map of your relationships with these people and groups, like the one above.

a Show which people are the most important for you. The larger the more important.

b Next to each circle, write:

- how much time you spend with them;
- an example of something that you do and something that you don't do with them.

► **Pronunciation: page 112**

3 How do you think your lifestyle map will change in the future?

Learning diary

1

1 In this unit you have revised ways of talking about the present and the future.

How well had you remembered these things?

What things had you forgotten? Discuss your answers with other members of your class.

2 What new things have you learnt in this unit? How well do you know them?

3 Do the self-check in the Workbook.

2 turning points

past tenses: revision

Contents

Learning objectives

In this unit you will revise the tenses that we use for talking about the past.

Preview task

What can you remember?

- What tenses can you use for talking about the past?
- Look through the unit. Find an example of each one.
- Write down two things that you know about each tense.

There is a new past tense in this unit. Look through the unit.

- Find an example of the tense.
- Find its name.

Sue's secret

1 What do you remember? What happened in the last part of the story? Look back at page 10 and check your ideas.

2 Look at this episode. Who are the people? Where are they? What are they doing?

3 Listen and follow in your books.

Kamala I didn't see Terry at the dance on Friday. Was he there?

Sue No, he didn't go. One of his friends at the office was having a party. But I don't care. I had a super weekend.

Kamala Why? What did you do? Come on, Sue. What's the secret?

Sue OK, Kam. Promise you won't tell anyone, but I met the most wonderful boy in the world.

Kamala Steady on, Sue. It's not like you to get excited. Who is this wonderful guy?

Sue You saw him on Friday. I was talking to him. His name's Joe.

Kamala Oh, yes. I remember – tall guy. I'd never seen him before. What were you talking about?

Sue Victoria Road, mostly. Anyway, I've seen him again since then.

Kamala How? Did he ask you out?

Sue No, it was on Saturday morning. I had just got off the bus – you know, by the trees – and I saw him.

Kamala What was he doing?

Sue He wasn't doing anything really. He was looking at the trees. Anyway, we said hello and then we went for a cup of coffee. And on Sunday we went to the pictures.

Kamala Have you told Terry about this?

Sue No, I haven't. I haven't seen him for a week and he hasn't telephoned since last Monday. Anyway, Terry is now ancient history for me.

Casey Did someone mention History?

Kamala Oh, hi, Casey.

Casey Have you done the History project, Sue?

Sue Yes, I did it yesterday.

Casey Oh, good. Can I have a look at it? I haven't started it yet.

Kamala Casey! You can't talk about homework now. Sue has reached a turning point in her life. She's got a new boyfriend. Ouch! That hurt.

What do you think?

- What will Casey and Kamala do?
- How will Terry feel, when he finds out?

4 Answer these questions.

a Why didn't Terry go to the dance?
b Where did he go?
c Why doesn't Sue care?
d Why is Kamala surprised at Sue?
e Where did Sue meet Joe?
f What were Joe and Sue doing at the dance?
g What was Joe doing when Sue saw him on Saturday?
h What did Sue do when she saw Joe?
i What did Sue and Joe do on Sunday?
j Why hasn't Sue told Terry?
k Why did Casey want to see Sue's project?
l Why did Kamala say that Suc has reached a turning point in her life?
m Why did Sue kick Kamala?

5 Close your book. Listen to the dialogue again.

Useful expressions

6 **How do you say these in your language?**

I don't care.	
super	
What's the secret?	
Steady on.	
It's not like you to . . .	
guy	
Did he ask you out?	
That's ancient history.	
She's reached a turning point in her life.	
Ouch!	

7 **Work in groups of three. Each person takes one of the parts. Read the dialogue.**

FOLLOW UP

8 **Write the answers to Exercise 4.**

LANGUAGE WORK

Talking about the past

1 **Look at the Victoria Road story. Four past tenses are used.**

a Complete the table with examples from the story.

b One of these tenses is new. Which one?

c Look at the new tense. What do you think it means? Translate it into your language.

Past simple	
statement	....
negative	....
question	....
Past continuous	
statement	....
negative	....
question	....
Present perfect	
statement	....
negative	....
question	....
Past perfect	
statement	....
negative	*Kamala hadn't seen Joe before Friday.*
question	....

Past simple and present perfect

2 Look at these sentences from the story.

a Complete the sentences.

I .... him for a week.

I .... Terry at the dance on Friday.

.... you .... the History project?

Yes, I .... it yesterday.

b What are the two tenses?

c Why are the tenses different?

3 What has Sue done since last Monday? Look at this list. Read the story and use her diary on page 16 to help you.

Example

She's been to a dance.
She hasn't seen Terry.

go to a dance	telephone Terry
see Terry	finish her History project
go to a birthday party	fall in love
meet Joe	tell Terry about Joe
have coffee with Joe	play badminton with Kamala
visit Joe's parents	do her community work
see a film	

4 Look at the things Sue has done. Say when she did them.

Example

She went to a dance on Friday.

5 Interview your partner. Look at the pictures. Find out whether he/she has done these things since last Monday. Ask questions to get more information.

a Decide what questions you will ask.

b Ask your questions.

Example

A *'Have you bought anything since last Monday?'*
B *'Yes, I have.'*
A *'What did you buy?'*
or *'How much did it cost?'*

telephoned someone

bought something

seen a film

played a sport

met someone interesting

been to a party

had an argument

fallen in love

FOLLOW UP

6 Write down six interesting things that you have done since last Monday. Say when you did each one.

READING

1066

1 Read the first paragraph and answer the questions.

a What year was it?
b What was happening?
c What was the problem?

2 Look at the map opposite. Identify these people.

Harold Godwin   Duke William   Harald Hardraada

3 The rest of the story about '1066' is in the wrong order.

a Read the texts and number them in the correct order.

b Explain how you worked out the order.

[1] The year was 1065 and in London the English king, Edward the Confessor, was dying. He had no children and three men claimed the throne of England: Harold Godwin, the Earl of Wessex, William, the Duke of Normandy and Harald Hardraada, the King of Norway.

[ ] The Normans attacked but the Anglo-Saxon soldiers were safe on the top of the hill. They pushed the Normans back. Then the Normans pretended to run away. Some of the Anglo-Saxons chased them down the hill. But the Norman knights turned round and killed them.

[ ] And that was all that Hardraada received. By the end of the day he was dead and the Norwegian army had been destroyed. But, while Harold and his soldiers were resting after the battle, news arrived from London: Duke William had landed on the south coast near the town of Hastings.

[ ] When the news reached Duke William, he was very angry. William was the Duke of Normandy in northern France and he was Edward's cousin. Edward had grown up in Normandy and he had promised William the throne. Duke William was tall and strong and he was a famous soldier.

[ ] After the Battle of Hastings, William marched to London and was crowned king of England. He is now called William the Conqueror and 1066 is the most famous date in English history. It was a turning point for English history and the English language.

[ ] William stayed near Hastings and waited for Harold Godwin. The English king returned to London, collected a new army and marched to Hastings. They stopped on a hill and the battle began. The Anglo-Saxons fought on foot, but the Normans were on horses.

[ ] Harold Godwin was the most important of the Anglo-Saxon lords. Edward had been a weak king and Harold had been the real ruler of England for many years. When Edward died at the end of 1065, Harold was crowned king.

[ ] Harold and most of his army had stayed on the hill. But then the Norman archers attacked. They fired their arrows into the air. King Harold looked up and an arrow hit him in the eye. The last Anglo-Saxon king was dead and Duke William had won.

[ ] But if William was tall, Harald Hardraada was even taller. He was a giant, almost seven feet tall. Hardraada's ancestors had been kings of England before Edward and now he wanted the throne for himself.

[ ] The Anglo-Saxon and Norwegian armies met at Stamford Bridge near the city of York. Before the battle, Hardraada asked King Harold: 'How much of England will you give me?' 'Seven feet,' Godwin replied, 'enough for your grave.'

[ ] The first challenge to King Harold Godwin came from the north. In 1066 at the end of the summer, Harald Hardraada landed in north-eastern England. Godwin marched north with his army.

4 **Draw arrows on the map to mark the movements of the three armies.**

Past perfect

5 **Look at this sentence.**

William was angry, because Edward had promised him the throne.

a Name the two tenses used in this sentence.

b The sentence describes two events in the past. Which one happened first?

William was angry.
Edward promised William the throne.

c Complete this rule.

> The ____________________ tense shows an event which happened ____________________ another event in the past.

6 **Answer these.**

a Explain why each of the three men claimed the throne.
b Why did Harold become king?
c What had King Harold Godwin done before he met Duke William at Hastings?
d How did the Normans win the Battle of Hastings?

WORD WORK

7 **Make a list of all the words associated with 'kings' and 'war'.**

FOLLOW UP

8 **Write down all the facts about the four men in the text.**

Edward the Confessor Harold Godwin
Duke William Harald Hardraada

LISTENING

And then he kissed me

Verse 1

Well he ________ up to me
and he ________ me if I ________ to dance.
He ________ kind of nice
and so I ________ I might take a chance.
When we ________ he ________ me tight.
And when he ________ me home that night
All the stars ________ ________ bright.
And then he ________ me.

Verse 2

The first time I ________ him
I ________ wait to see him again.
I ________ to let him know
that I ________ more than a friend.
I ________ ________ just what to do
So I ________ I ________ you.
And he ________ that he ________ me, too.
And then he ________ me.

Chorus

He ________ me in a way
that I'd never ________ before.
He ________ me in a way
that I ________ to be kissed for evermore.

Verse 3

I ________ that he ________ mine
so I ________ him all the love that I ________.
And one day he ________ me home
to meet his Mom and his Dad.
Then he ________ me to ________ his bride
And always ________ right by his side.
I ________ so happy that I almost ________.
And then he ________ me.

1 **Listen to this song. Have you ever heard it before? Fill in the missing verbs in the correct tense. Use the verbs below.**

love be dance ask feel look can
whisper see walk hold cry think know
want shine give kiss take have say

2 **Imagine a boy is singing the song. How does it change?**

Past simple and past continuous: revision

3 **Look at these two sentences from the song.**

He **walked** up to me and he **asked**
me if I wanted to dance.

When he **walked** me home that night
All the stars **were shining** bright.

a What tenses are used in the sentences?

b Why are the tenses different in the second sentence?

c Find more examples in the Victoria Road story on page 20.

FOLLOW UP

4 **Ask your parents or grandparents how they first met. Write their story.**

INTERACTION

A turning point

In this unit you have learnt about a turning point in Sue's life and a turning point in English history. What about your life?

1 **What turning points have there been in your life? Think about things or people that have changed your life.**

2 **Ask your partner about important turning points in his or her life.**

a What questions will you ask?

Example
What happened?
What were you doing?
How has it changed your life?

b Interview your partner. Find out as much as you can.

3 **Report your findings to the class. Are there any common turning points in people's lives?**

FOLLOW UP

4 **Write about an important turning point in your life.**

✻ In a doctor's waiting room

Patient: The doctor says I've got to take one of these tablets every day for the rest of my life.

Friend: Well don't worry. That's not too bad.

Patient: Yes, but he's only given me six tablets.

PROJECT

Your country's history

1066 is the most famous date in English history. It was an important turning point.

Write about the most famous date in your country's history.

a What happened?

b Why did it happen?

c What effects has it had?

The first atomic bomb tests were carried out in America during the second world war. The first atomic bomb was dropped on Hiroshima in Japan on 6 August 1945.

The first Europeans arrive in America in 1492.

The Greeks defeated the Persian invasion in 427 BC at the Battle of Marathon.

Garibaldi enters Rome during the campaigns to unify Italy (1848 - 61).

In November 1989 the Berlin Wall came down after 28 years. This led to the unification of Germany a year later.

The storming of the Bastille on 14 July 1789 was the start of the French Revolution.

Learning diary

2

1 In this unit you have revised ways of talking about the past and learnt a new tense.

How well do you know these things?

2 Do the self-check in the Workbook.

3 Compare the English past tenses with your own language. What differences are there?

What do you find difficult about the English tenses?

Discuss your answers with other members of your class.

► **Pronunciation: page 112**

3 people

the conditional; 'if' clauses

Contents

Learning objectives

In this unit you will learn how to:

- express conditions
- ask what people would choose
- describe personality and appearance
- describe the patterns, shapes and colours of clothes
- say what kind of people you admire or dislike

Preview task

There is a new tense in this unit.

- Find an example of the tense.
- Find its name.
- What do you think it means?

How can I tell him?

1 What do you remember? What happened in the last part of the story? Look back at page 20 and check your ideas.

2 Look at this episode. Who are the people? Where are they? What are they doing?

3 Listen and follow in your books.

Vince What's he like, your new boyfriend?

Sue Well, he's twenty-two and he's quite tall. He's got dark hair and lovely blue eyes.

Vince He's a bit old for you, isn't he?

Sue You sound like Dad. That's just what he would say.

Vince What does he do?

Sue I don't know. But he's a really interesting guy.

Vince Terry phoned again today. You must tell him, you know. You wouldn't like it, if he did the same thing to you.

Sue I know, Vince, but . . . . Oh, I don't know. What would you do, if you were me?

Vince If I were you, I'd tell him the truth – and the sooner the better.

Sue Oh, I couldn't do that. It would hurt him.

Vince Well, he'll find out sooner or later. And it would be better if he heard it from you.

Sue I suppose you're right. But I can't do anything about it now or I'll be late for work.

Later

Man You look very pretty today, my dear.

Sue I've got a new boyfriend, Mr Jones. We're going to a party tonight.

Man If I was fifty years younger, nobody else would stand a chance.

Sue Go on with you, Mr Jones.

Later

Terry Hello, Sue. Vince said I'd find you here.

Sue Oh, hello, Terry.

Terry Look, I'm sorry about the other evening. It was a terrible party, anyway. Would you like to go out this evening?

Sue This evening? Oh, I can't. I'm ... er ... I'm washing my hair.

Joe Hi, Sue. Jump in.

Sue Terry, this is Joe.

What do you think?

- What would you do if you were Terry?
- What would you do if you were Sue?
- What do you think about Joe?

4 Right, Wrong or Don't know?

	✓	✖	?
a Sue has told Vince about Joe.	❑	❑	❑
b Joe works in an office.	❑	❑	❑
c Terry has phoned Sue more than once.	❑	❑	❑
d Sue doesn't want to tell Terry about Joe.	❑	❑	❑
e Sue is doing her community work today.	❑	❑	❑
f Terry didn't know that Sue was at the hospital.	❑	❑	❑
g Sue is washing her hair this evening.	❑	❑	❑
h Joe is driving his father's car.	❑	❑	❑

5 Close your book. Listen to the dialogue again.

Useful expressions

6 **How do you say these in your language?**

What's he like?	
You sound like ...	
That's what he would say.	
You wouldn't like it if ...	
If I were you, I'd ...	
tell him the truth	
the sooner the better	
sooner or later	
I suppose you're right.	
I'll be late for ...	
They wouldn't stand a chance.	
Go on with you.	
Jump in.	

7 **Work in groups of four. One person is Vince, one is Sue, one is Terry and one is Joe and the man. Read the dialogue.**

FOLLOW UP

8 **Kamala is talking to Casey. Complete their conversation.**

Casey How old is Sue's new boyfriend?

Kamala Twenty-two, I think.

Casey He's .... bit old .... Sue, isn't ....? What .... he do?

Kamala I don't know.

Casey .... she told Terry yet?

Kamala No, she hasn't. I .... tell him, ... I was her. He'll find out .... or later and it would .... better if he .... it from Sue.

Casey Yes, I .... you're right, but I .... like to do it.

LANGUAGE WORK

The conditional tense

1 **Look at this sentence.**

It **would hurt** him.

We call this **the conditional tense**.

a Find more examples of the conditional tense from the Victoria Road story.

b Choose examples from the story to complete this table.

Full form	Short form
statement	statement ....
negative *You would not like it.*	negative ....
question	

£20,000 . . . .

2 **What would you do with £20,000?**

a Write down your ideas.

b Work with a partner and compare your ideas.

c Look at the pictures opposite. What would those people do with £20,000?

'If' clauses

3 Look at the sentences from the story.

a Complete them.

You .... it, if he .... the same thing to you.

What .... you ...., if you .... me?

It .... better, if he .... it from you.

If I ....
fifty years younger,
nobody else .... a chance.

b What tense is used:

- in the main clause?
- in the 'If' clause?

4 Put the verbs in brackets into the correct form.

a If I .... £10,000, I .... a new car. (have/buy)

b If Sue .... Terry the truth, it .... better. (tell/be)

c Terry .... it, if he .... from someone else. (not like/find out)

d If Sue .... with Terry, Joe .... angry. (go out/be)

e If I .... Terry, I .... (be/not care)

f Terry .... in trouble, if he .... Joe. (be/hit)

g If I .... two years older, I .... school. (be/leave)

FOLLOW UP

5 Write the answers to Exercise 2c.

If all the people in China
stood on each other's shoulders,
they would reach to the moon
and back twice.

READING

1 Here's a personality test.

a Read the questions and tick the correct box in the personality profile.

b Compare your answers with a partner.

c How did you score? Check at the bottom of page 35.

What kind of person are you?

Do you like to be the centre of attention or do you prefer to be on your own? Do you like to be the leader or do you prefer to be part of a team? Are you confident, quiet, bossy, sensitive? Find out more about yourself from the personality test.

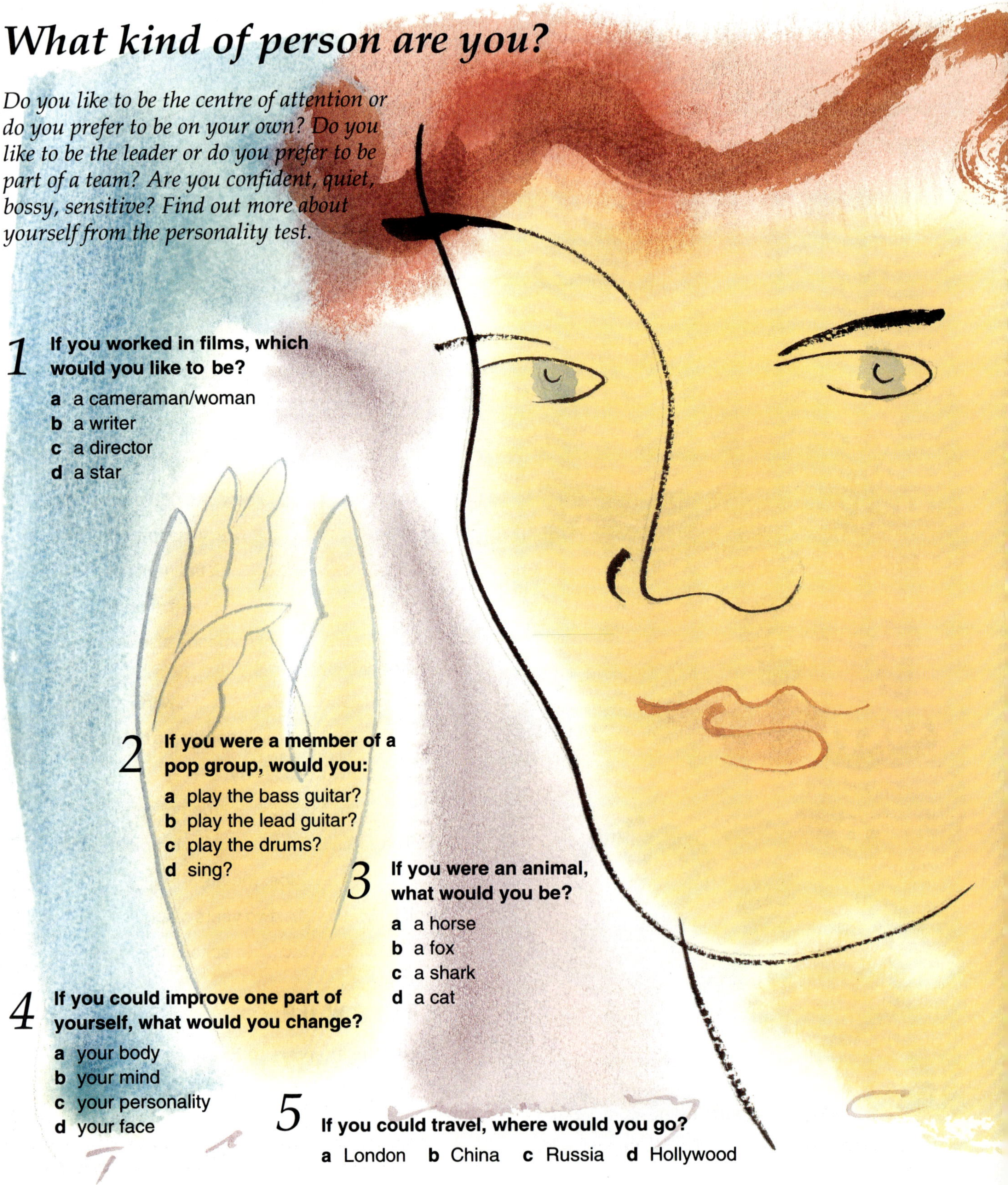

1 If you worked in films, which would you like to be?

a a cameraman/woman
b a writer
c a director
d a star

2 If you were a member of a pop group, would you:

a play the bass guitar?
b play the lead guitar?
c play the drums?
d sing?

3 If you were an animal, what would you be?

a a horse
b a fox
c a shark
d a cat

4 If you could improve one part of yourself, what would you change?

a your body
b your mind
c your personality
d your face

5 If you could travel, where would you go?

a London **b** China **c** Russia **d** Hollywood

★★★ PERSONALITY PROFILE ★★★										
★	1	2	3	4	5	6	7	8	9	10
a										
b										
c										
d										

6 If you went to live in another country, which would you miss most?

- **a** your family
- **b** your possessions
- **c** your language
- **d** your friends

7 If you won some money, what would you buy?

- **a** something useful
- **b** records and books
- **c** presents for other people
- **d** clothes

8 If you were on a desert island and could only have one thing, what would you take with you?

a a knife **b** a book **c** a dog **d** a mirror

9 If you were on a desert island with one other person, who would you choose?

- **a** a doctor
- **b** a famous scientist
- **c** a politician
- **d** a film star

10 Which of these would you most like to be?

a loved **b** free **c** rich **d** famous

Conditional tense: questions

2 Look at the questions in the personality test.

a Complete the rule.

> To make questions in the conditional tense, we put ____________ in front of ____________.

b Complete these questions with the verbs in brackets.

If you found a lot of money, ...

.... ? (do/you/what/would)

....? (you/tell/would/the police)

WORD WORK

3 Find all the names of jobs in the personality test.

a Write them down.

b How many more can you think of in one minute?

4 Report your scores of the personality profile to the class. Make a classroom profile. How many people were in each personality type?

FOLLOW UP

5 Write your answers to the personality test.

Example

If I worked in films, I would like to be a director.

How did you score?

Did you score mostly 'a's? You are a very practical person. You don't like to work alone and you like to help people. If your dreams came true, you would be a doctor or an engineer.

Did you score mostly 'c's? You are a natural manager. You like to direct other people. In your dreams you would be a politician, a football manager or a business executive.

Did you score mostly 'b's? You are a loner. You are interested in ideas. You like to be free and to work on your own. You don't like to be on the stage. In your dreams you would be a writer or an artist.

Did you score mostly 'd's? You are an 'I' person. You think a lot about your image. You like to be the centre of attention. If your dreams came true, you would be a film star, a pop star or a model.

Was no letter dominant? You have a balanced personality.

LISTENING

Dress sense

1 Read this.

What is your dress sense like? Do all clothes suit you? Can you wear any style or colour you like and still look good? For most of us, the answer is no. We have to choose our clothes carefully to suit ourselves and the shape of our body. This goes for boys and girls.

a What is it about?

b Is it just for girls?

c What will follow it?

2 What is your dress sense like? What do you think the basic rules are?

3 Listen. Which of these are mentioned?

leather clothes	big things	tartans
light colours	small things	stripes
dark clothes	tight clothes	loose styles
patterns	high heels	checks

4 Listen again. What effect does each have?

5 Look at these pictures of Hannah and Peter. They are each wearing three of their favourite outfits.

a Describe their outfits.

b What effect does each outfit have?

Example

The . . . makes him/her look slimmer/broader.

c Which outfit do you think they look best in?

d What about you? What kind of clothes do you prefer?

WORD WORK

6 Make a list of the words that are used to describe 'people' and 'things'. Then listen again and check your lists.

FOLLOW UP

7 Complete this.

Patterns make things look .... So if you are .... as slim as you .... like to be, wear .... colours or choose .... patterns. Be very careful with .... If you are tall .... thin, don't wear .... stripes. You'll look like .... lamp post. A T-shirt .... horizontal stripes, on the other hand, has the .... effect. It will .... your shoulders look .... That's good news for all you guys who want .... shoulders. But girls, if .... want a narrower .... , don't wear clothers with .... stripes.

INTERACTION

Terry and Joe

1 Look at the final scene of the Victoria Road story on page 30. What do you think happens next? What would you do in this situation? Here are some possible ideas. Can you think of any more?

- Sue tries to explain to Terry, while Joe is there.
- Sue doesn't go with Joe. She goes home with Terry.
- Terry leaves. The next day he meets Sue in the street.
- Terry leaves. He goes to the leisure centre. Kamala, Casey and Vince are there.

2 Write an episode about what happens next.

a Decide what happens.

b Make sure there is a role for every member of your group.

c Write the dialogue for the scene.

3 Act your dialogue.

FOLLOW UP

4 Write a short summary of your play.

PROJECT

Mother Theresa

Michelle Pfeiffer

Mikhail Gorbachev

Sting and Raoni

Nelson Mandela

Heroes and heroines

What kind of people do you admire? What kind of people do you dislike?

a Collect pictures of people that you admire and people you dislike.

b Arrange your pictures into a collage.

c Write about each person. Say why you admire him/her or why you dislike him/her.

d Would you like to be like any of the people you described? Why?

Our local youth worker

My Uncle

Arantxa Sanchez

Giorgio Armani

Learning diary

3

1 What have you learnt in this unit? Look at the first page of the unit. How well have you achieved the learning objectives?

2 Do the self-check in the Workbook.

3 Look at the activities in units 1 to 3. Which activities did you like best? Write down your three favourite activities. Why did you like them? Discuss your answers with other members of your class.

▶ **Pronunciation: page 113**

revision 4

READING

1 Who is the girl in the picture? Read the text quickly and find out the following information.

a What is her name?	b Where is she from?	c What is she?
Madge Mitchell	England	a dancer
Kylie Minogue	New Zealand	an actress
Little Eva	Wales	a singer
Charlene Robinson	Australia	a model

Star Profile

A few years ago, the BBC bought a cheap Australian soap opera called *Neighbours*. At first it was shown at lunchtime, but during the school holidays it became very popular with kids. When school started again, the programme's young fans did anything to see their favourite programme. Some went home at lunchtime (or to a friend's house). The BBC's Controller of Programmes was Michael Grade. He heard from his daughter, Alison, that she and her friends watched the programme secretly in the school's computer room. So the BBC showed the programme again at 5pm after school finishes. Now every day in Britain, the show has an audience that is bigger than the total population of Australia.

One of the stars of the show is Kylie Minogue. She plays the part of Charlene Robinson. *Neighbours* was Kylie's big break. In 1987 she was the most popular actress in Australia. Since then, she has started a new career as a pop singer with number one hits in Australia and in the UK. Her first record 'The Locomotion' was a remake of an old sixties hit by Little Eva. It was number one in Australia for seven weeks. Her second record 'I Should Be So Lucky' stayed at the top of the British charts for five weeks.

Before *Neighbours*, Kylie had had a few small parts in other Australian shows. Her first part was in 1979 when she was only eleven years old. She had a part in a soap opera called *The Sullivans*. But after that she did nothing till 1984 when she started work in *The Henderson Kids*. In 1985 she got a part in *The Zoo Family*.

Neighbours is about three families who live in Ramsey Street, Melbourne. Kylie plays the strong-willed and impatient Charlene — Madge Mitchell's daughter. She first appeared in 1986 as Charlene Mitchell. She and her boyfriend, Scott Robinson (played by Jason Donovan) quickly became the stars of the show. When Charlene and Scott got married in 1987, the whole of Australia celebrated the wedding.

Kylie is now at a turning point in her career. She has left *Neighbours* and has made her first film, *Delinquents*. Where will she go next? One thing is certain, in the next few years we'll see a lot more of this attractive young woman from down under.

2 Right, Wrong or Don't know?

		✓	✖	?
a	Neighbours is made in Britain.	❏	❏	❏
b	It is the most popular TV show in Australia.	❏	❏	❏
c	Alison Grade is a Neighbours fan.	❏	❏	❏
d	Neighbours is not shown at lunchtime now.	❏	❏	❏
e	Kylie Minogue played Charlene Mitchell.	❏	❏	❏
f	Only three families live in Ramsey Street.	❏	❏	❏
g	Charlene was Kylie's first part in a TV show.	❏	❏	❏
h	'The Locomotion' was first recorded by Little Eva.	❏	❏	❏
i	'I Should Be So Lucky' was number one in Australia.	❏	❏	❏
j	Kylie married Jason Donovan in 1987.	❏	❏	❏
k	Kylie has gone to live in America.	❏	❏	❏

3 Kylie's career

a Put these in the correct order.

☐ The Henderson Kids	☐ Delinquents
☐ Neighbours	☐ The Sullivans
☐ I Should Be So Lucky	☐ The Locomotion
☐ Mrs Robinson	☐ The Zoo Family

b The text tells you the dates for most of these. Write them down and work out the approximate years for the others.

c How important was each of these in Kylie's career?

4 Say whether the following facts are about Kylie or Charlene.

She has had number one hits in Australia and the UK.
She is a singer.
She married Scott Robinson.
She has a mother called Madge.
She has left Neighbours.
She lives in Ramsey Street.
She appeared in The Henderson Kids.
She lives in Melbourne.
She is impatient.
She was born in 1968.

5 What do you think?

a How do you feel when you read about Kylie? Do you think she is lucky? Do you feel jealous? Would you like to do something similar?

b What is your favourite soap opera? When is it on? Why do you like it?

c If you could be someone in a TV show, who would you be? Why?

FOLLOW UP

6 Look at your answers to Exercises 1, 3 and 4. Write about Kylie Minogue's career.

Characters from *Neighbours*

LISTENING

Soap operas

1 **Listen. You will hear a girl talking about her favourite soap opera. Tick the correct information.**

a What is her favourite programme?

Brookside	Home and Away
Dallas	Coronation Street

b Where is the programme from?

Britain	the United States
Australia	Canada

c Who is her favourite character?

Norman	Curly
Shorty	Kimberly

d How does she describe him?

He's got curly hair.	He's good-looking.
He's short.	He wears glasses.

e Why does she like him?

He's clever.	He's romantic.
He's kind.	He's funny.
He's serious.	

2 **Listen again and find the answers to these questions.**

a When is the programme on?

b What is it about?

c How old is the girl's favourite character?

d Where does he work?

e Why does she think he's funny?

3 **Interview your partner about his/her favourite soap opera. Use questions like these.**

- What is your favourite soap opera?
- What country is it from?
- Who is your favourite character?
- What is he/she like?
- Why do you like him/her?

FOLLOW UP

4 **Write about your favourite soap opera.**

PROJECT

Your favourite TV show

1 **Work in groups. Think of your favourite TV show. Imagine you are the writers and invent a new character. Describe him/her.**

a What does he/she look like?

b What kind of character has he/she got?

c What is his/her relationship to other characters in the show?

d What is his/her background?

2 **Write the scene when he/she first appears in the show. Try to use some of the Useful expressions from Units 1 to 3.**

3 **Act your scene.**

► **Pronunciation: page 113**

5 protest

the passive: revision

Contents

Learning objectives

In this unit you will revise the passive voice.
You will also learn how to:

- express cause and effect
- classify things
- ask about and express opinions
- talk about issues that you care about
- understand slogans

Preview task

In this unit you will learn about an important international problem.

- Look through the unit. What is the problem?
- What do you already know about this problem?

Save our trees

1 What do you remember? What happened in the last part of the story? Look back at page 30 and check your ideas.

2 Look at this episode. Who are the people? What is the demonstration about? What do Terry and Joe do? What happens to Sue and Terry?

3 Listen and follow in your books.

Casey Are you coming to the demo on Saturday?

Terry What demo?

Casey Don't you ever read anything, Terry? Look at this leaflet. Kam wrote it, you know.

Terry 'Save Our Trees. Last week permission was given for the Kingman Property Company to cut down the old trees at the end of Victoria Road. The land is needed for new offices and flats. Those trees are nearly two hundred years old. They were planted in the time of Napoleon. Unless we do something, they will be cut down next week and two hundred years of history will be destroyed. Letters have been written to the local council and a petition has been organized. A demonstration will be held at the trees on Saturday 20th at 9.30 am. Please come along and support us. Save our trees.'

Are you going?

Casey We all are. I've already made a placard. Vince and Sue have made a big banner.

On Saturday

All Save our trees. Save our trees.

Sue Will you sign our petition, please?

Joe Hi, Sue. Can I join you?

Sue Yes, sure. The more the merrier.

Joe Here, I'll take that.

Terry No, you won't.

Sue Come on, Terry. Let Joe help.

Terry You don't live around here. Now let go of this pole.

Joe Hey, who are you pushing?

Later

Mr Scott Kamala, what on earth is the matter?

Kamala Oh, Mr Scott. There's been a fight. Sue and Terry have been taken to the police station. They've been arrested.

What do you think?

- Who started the fight?
- What do you think about the protest?

4 Right, Wrong or Don't know?

	✓	✖	?
a Terry already knew about the demonstration.	❑	❑	❑
b The leaflet was written by Kamala.	❑	❑	❑
c Only four of the trees will be cut down.	❑	❑	❑
d The trees were planted by Napoleon.	❑	❑	❑
e Some new houses will be built by the local council.	❑	❑	❑
f The demonstration has been organized by Casey.	❑	❑	❑
g The petition has been signed by a thousand people.	❑	❑	❑
h The demonstration will be held on Saturday morning.	❑	❑	❑
i Joe wants to hold the banner.	❑	❑	❑
j Casey and Joe are arrested.	❑	❑	❑

5 Close your book. Listen to the dialogue again.

Useful expressions

6 **How do you say these in your language?**

a demo	
the local council	
Please come along and support us.	
a petition	
a placard	
a banner	
Can I join you?	
the more the merrier	
Here, I'll take that.	
Let go of it.	
What on earth is the matter?	
They've been arrested.	

7 **Work in groups of four. One person is Terry, one is Joe, one is Casey and Mr Scott, and one is Sue and Kamala. Read the dialogue.**

FOLLOW UP

8 **A reporter is asking Casey questions about the demonstration. Here are the reporter's questions. Give Casey's answers.**

a Why will the trees be cut down?
b Who will cut them down?
c Why shouldn't they cut the trees down?
d When were the trees planted?
e Who have you written to?
f What else have you done?
g When was your demonstration?
h What happened at the demonstration?
i Who started the fight?
j What has happened to them?

LANGUAGE WORK

The passive

1 **What do you know about the passive?**

a Look at these two sentences. Which one has the passive verb?

Kamala wrote the leaflet.
Letters have been written to the local council.

b Find more examples of the passive in the Victoria Road story. Put them in a chart like this.

Past

....
....
....

Present perfect

....
....
....

Present

....
....
....

Future

....
....
....

c Do you remember how the passive is made? Complete the rule.

We make the passive with the verb ________ and the ________ participle.

2 When do we use the passive?

It is not easy to answer this question. Here is a general rule.

> **We use the passive when the action is more important than the agent.**

a Look at the two sentences in 1a.

In the first example, **the agent** is the most important part of the sentence.

Who wrote the leaflet?
Kamala wrote it.

In the second example, the most important part of the sentence is **the action.**

What has happened?
Letters **have been written.**

It does not matter who has written them.

b Look at the sentences in your chart. Do they follow this rule?

3 Casey and Kamala are planning the protest about the trees. Here is their list.

- *organize a petition* ✓
- *paint posters*
- *write letters to the local council* ✓
- *hold a demonstration*
- *make banners and placards* ✓
- *print a leaflet* ✓
- *deliver the leaflets*
- *ask people to join the demonstration* ✓
- *invite the local radio to the demonstration*
- *inform the police about the demonstration* ✓
- *send the petition to the local council*

a Look at the list and say what will be done.

Example
A petition will be organized.

b It is now a few days before the demonstration. Casey and Kamala are checking their list. Ask and answer what has been done.

Kamala *Has a petition been organized?*

Casey *Yes, it has.*

Kamala *Have posters been painted?*

Casey *No, they haven't.*

FOLLOW UP

4 Write the answers to Exercises 3 a and b.

······ *Culture* spot ······

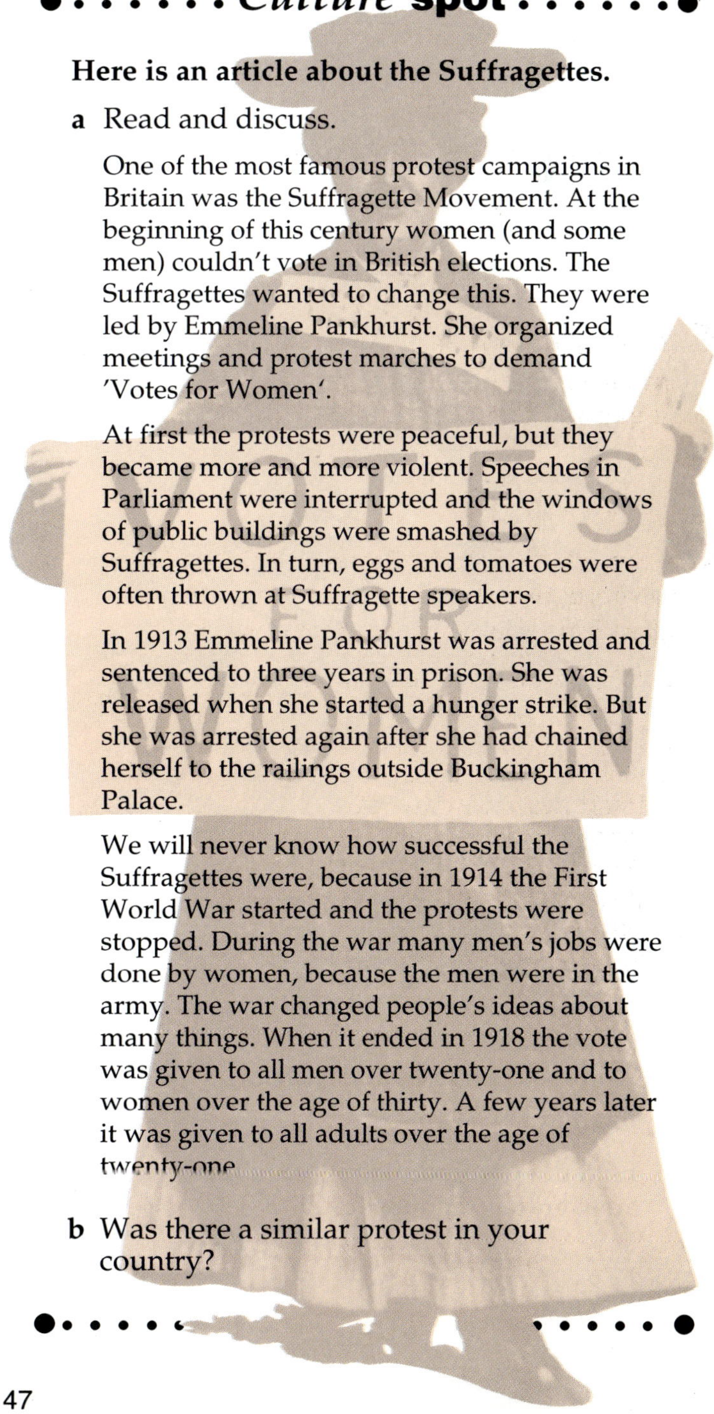

Here is an article about the Suffragettes.

a Read and discuss.

One of the most famous protest campaigns in Britain was the Suffragette Movement. At the beginning of this century women (and some men) couldn't vote in British elections. The Suffragettes wanted to change this. They were led by Emmeline Pankhurst. She organized meetings and protest marches to demand 'Votes for Women'.

At first the protests were peaceful, but they became more and more violent. Speeches in Parliament were interrupted and the windows of public buildings were smashed by Suffragettes. In turn, eggs and tomatoes were often thrown at Suffragette speakers.

In 1913 Emmeline Pankhurst was arrested and sentenced to three years in prison. She was released when she started a hunger strike. But she was arrested again after she had chained herself to the railings outside Buckingham Palace.

We will never know how successful the Suffragettes were, because in 1914 the First World War started and the protests were stopped. During the war many men's jobs were done by women, because the men were in the army. The war changed people's ideas about many things. When it ended in 1918 the vote was given to all men over twenty-one and to women over the age of thirty. A few years later it was given to all adults over the age of twenty-one.

b Was there a similar protest in your country?

READING

The disappearing rain forest

1 Look at the title and the pictures.

a What is the text about?

b What do you know about the problem?

2 Read these questions.

- Why are the forests being destroyed? (two reasons)
- Who is to blame?
- What other problem does the destruction of the forest cause?
- Why won't new forests be planted?

a Read the text quickly.

b Find the paragraph that contains the answer to each question.

3 Read the text and find the answers.

1 Before the end of this lesson another hectare of the world's forests will be destroyed forever. Why is this happening? There are two reasons - land and wood. In many countries the trees have been cut down because the land was needed for animals or crops. In other parts of the world the trees are cut down because their wood is wanted. This wood is used by the local people for firewood. Or it is exported to Japan, Europe and North America. There it is used for buildings or it is made into furniture.

2 Unfortunately, in most places the trees won't be replaced. The soil in the forests is very thin, but it is protected by the trees. When the trees are cut down, the soil is washed away by the rain or blown away by the wind. Soon nothing can be grown on it. The forest becomes a desert. Then more land will be needed and more trees will be cut down.

3 When the forest is destroyed, it isn't only the trees that are lost, the homes of millions of animals and plants are destroyed, too. At the moment there are between five and ten million species of animals and plants on the Earth. By the year 2000, one million of these will be extinct - that's one species every hour. All kinds of species are in danger - fish, reptiles, birds, mammals, insects and shellfish - as well as thousands of plants.

4 Who is to blame for this disaster? The answer is simple: all of us. There are just too many people in the world. The world's population is now over one billion people. Of course, it's very easy to blame the local people. We don't chop down trees. They do. But the products are bought by people like you and me - the hi-fi with its teak loudspeakers, or the nice mahogany chairs. Why are the forests being destroyed? Just look around. You're probably sitting on it or listening to it.

WORD WORK

4 Look at this sentence.

But the products are bought by people like you and me – the hi-fi with its teak loudspeakers, or the nice mahogany chairs.

a What are 'teak' and 'mahogany'?

countries
kinds of animals
kinds of wood
kinds of trees
colours

How do you know?

b The text mentions six kinds of animals. Find the names and write them as headings in this chart.

....	....	....	....	....	....
....	....	....	....	....	....
....	....	....	....	....	....
....	....	....	....	....	....
....	....	....	....	....	....
....	....	....	....	....	....

c Use a dictionary. Find the names of five animals for each column.

5 What do you think about the problem of the forests? Do you think you are to blame?

FOLLOW UP

6 In many countries forests, fields and marshes are being destroyed. Is this a problem in your country?

a Find out if your country has a policy to protect the environment.

b Write about what you find out.

LISTENING

The Penans

© Payne/Survival International

1 Look at the picture. What do you think?

a Who are the people?

b Where are they?

c What are they doing?

How do you feel about these people? Do they look friendly?

2 Listen.

a Find the answers to the questions.

b How do you feel about the people now?

3 Listen again. Write down three things:

- that have already happened to the forest;
- that the Penans have done;
- that will happen, if the forest is destroyed.

The publisher wishes to thank Survival International for the use of the photograph above.

4 Read the quotations.

a Who do you think these things were said by?

'We are poor people, too. We do our job and we earn our money.'

'There are plenty of trees here. We won't cut them all down.'

'Sarawak is a poor country. We have to export timber.'

'The jungle is our home. We must fight to save it.'

'The Penans are right. They are defending their home against corrupt politicians and greedy companies.'

'This is our problem. We don't need advice from the West.'

b What do you think the United Nations will say?

5 What do you think?

- Who would you support?
- What would you do if you were a Penan?

FOLLOW UP

6 Write the Penans' letter to the United Nations.

INTERACTION

Protest

1 Look at these protest posters.

a What are they about?

b How do you feel about these things? Do you care? Would you join a demonstration about them?

2 What do you care about? Work in groups. Discuss the questions below.

- Have you ever joined a demonstration?
- Would you join a demonstration about any of the issues on this page?
- Would you give money to support any of these protests?
- What else would you join a demonstration about?

3 Report your ideas to the class. What issues do people care about?

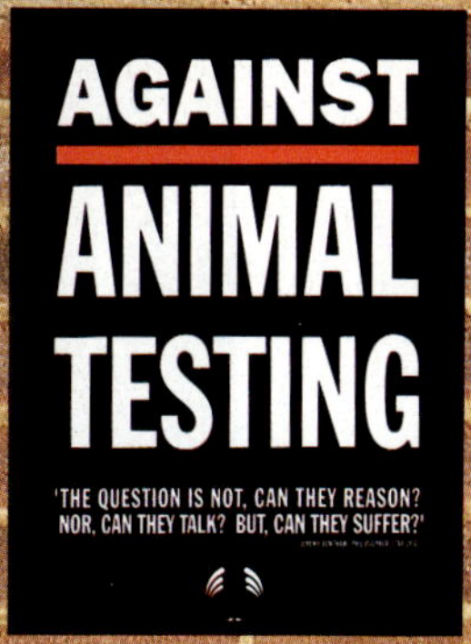

FOLLOW UP

4 Look at the text on page 48. Revise it for a dictation.

PROJECT

A protest campaign

Prepare a campaign about an issue that you feel strongly about.

a Make a leaflet on the issue. Write some facts and say what must be done. Illustrate it.

b Write a letter to the authorities and explain your campaign.

c Make a poster about your campaign.

water pollution

animal abuse

famine

industrial pollution

▶ **Pronunciation: page 113**

Learning diary 5

1 What have you learnt in this unit? Look at the first page of the unit. How well have you achieved the learning objectives?

2 Do the self-check in the Workbook.

3 Mistakes are a natural part of learning.
Look at your work for this unit. What mistakes have you made? Note down five.
Why do you think you made these mistakes?
Discuss your answers with other members of your class.

6 danger

gerunds; should/shouldn't

Contents

Learning objectives

In this unit you will learn how to:

- talk about activities
- give advice
- express risks
- compare risks and benefits
- describe illness
- answer a doctor's questions
- understand a diagnosis and treatment

Preview task

The theme of this unit is Danger. Look through the unit. What kinds of dangers will you learn about?

Sue goes hang-gliding

1 What do you remember? What happened in the last part of the story? Look back at page 44 and check your ideas.

2 Look at this episode. Who are the people? Where are they? What are they doing? What happens to Sue? Who is the girl at the airport?

3 Listen and follow in your books.

Mr Scott Hang-gliding? That's a bit dangerous, isn't it?

Sue Well, I'm not doing it myself. I'm only watching.

Mr Scott Is there anything that Joe does not do?

Sue Oh, he's got so many hobbies – horse riding, sailing . . .

Vince Snake charming, shark fishing, crocodile wrestling . . .

Sue Shut up, Vince. You're just jealous.

Mr Scott Well, you shouldn't forget things like doing your homework and passing exams, too, Sue. And what about meeting Carmen at the airport tomorrow?

Sue There's plenty of time. Her plane doesn't arrive till half past three.

Mr Scott Well, you should be at the airport by three.

Sue It's all right. Joe is giving me a lift. Oh, come on, Dad, please.

The next day

Girl Do you like hang-gliding?

Sue I don't know. I've never done it – but it looks like fun.

Joe Do you want to have a go?

Sue Oh, well, I don't know, er . . . OK.

Later

Sue Hey, how do I get down again? Help!

Joe Oh no, she's crashed!

Girl Quick.

Sue I think I've broken something.

At the airport

'British Airways announce the arrival of flight BA435 from Madrid.'

What do you think?

- What has happened to Sue?
- Will she get to the airport in time to meet Carmen?

4 Right, Wrong or Don't know?

	✓	✗	?
a Sue is going sailing tomorrow.	❑	❑	❑
b Carmen is arriving from Spain tomorrow.	❑	❑	❑
c Vince likes Joe.	❑	❑	❑
d Joe goes fishing.	❑	❑	❑
e Carmen is travelling by train.	❑	❑	❑
f Sue's father is taking her to the airport.	❑	❑	❑
g Sue's father is worried about Sue's schoolwork.	❑	❑	❑
h Sue doesn't like hang-gliding.	❑	❑	❑
i Sue breaks her leg when she crashes.	❑	❑	❑
j Carmen's plane is on time.	❑	❑	❑

5 Close your book. Listen to the dialogue again.

Useful expressions

6 **How do you say these in your language?**

a bit dangerous	
You're just jealous.	
There's plenty of time.	
It doesn't arrive till ...	
He's giving me a lift.	
Do you like ...ing?	
It looks like fun.	
Do you want to have a go?	
Help!	
She's crashed.	
I've broken something.	

7 **Work in groups of four. One person is Mr Scott, one is Sue, one is Vince and Joe and one is the other two parts.**

a Read the dialogue.

b Change roles and read the dialogue again.

FOLLOW UP

8 **Joe is at the hospital. He is talking to a doctor. Complete their conversation.**

Doctor Does she go .... often?

Joe No. She's never .... it before. She wanted to .... a go. Then she couldn't .... down again and she ....

Doctor She said something about .... and the airport.

Joe Oh no! I'd forgotten about .... Carmen. She's Sue's .... from Spain. She's coming to .... today. I was giving Sue a .... to the ....

Doctor What time does the plane .... ?

Joe Half .... three, I think.

Doctor Well, ... quarter to five now. I think you .... telephone the airport.

LANGUAGE WORK

Gerunds

1 **Look at these sentences.**

Hang-gliding is dangerous.
Do you like **hang-gliding**?

a We call this **-ing** form **a gerund**. It can be used as the subject or object of a sentence. Find more examples of gerunds in the story.

b What kind of word is 'hang-gliding'?

a verb   an adjective   a noun

c Translate the sentences above into your own language.

2 **Look at this list of activities.**

dancing	talking on the telephone
skiing	writing letters
swimming	watching television
sunbathing	playing football
learning English	doing housework
jogging	listening to the radio
sleeping	getting up in the morning
eating	taking photographs
reading	going shopping

a How do you feel about these activities? Put them in a chart like this.

	dancing	skiing	swimming	
I really like it.				
I like it.				
It's all right.				
I don't like it.				
I hate it.				

b Ask your partner whether he/she likes each activity.

Example
A *Do you like skiing?*
B *Yes, I do.* (or *It's all right.* or *No, I don't.*)

3 The most dangerous hobby in the world

a What does Vince say are Joe's hobbies? Label these pictures.

b Work in groups. Discuss these questions and write down your ideas.

What is the most dangerous hobby in the world?
What is the easiest job in the world?
What is the most boring activity in the world?
What is the most difficult thing in the world?
What is the most exciting hobby in the world?

c Compare your ideas to other groups' ideas. Vote for the best answers.

Giving advice

4 Look at the Victoria Road story again.

a Complete these sentences.

You .... forget things like doing your homework.

You .... be at the airport by three o'clock.

b Translate the sentences into your own language.

5 What should Carmen do?

a Say whether Carmen should or shouldn't do these things.

stay at the airport
telephone her parents
get a taxi to Sue's home
telephone Sue
ask someone for a lift
go back to Spain
ask at the information desk
find a hotel
leave the airport
take the train to Hartfield
ask a policeman for help
cry

b Explain your choice.

FOLLOW UP

6 Look at your chart for Exercise 2a. Write your answers in full sentences.

Example
I don't like skiing.
I really like swimming.
Sunbathing is all right.

READING

Danger

1 **Look at this list. It shows the risks of dying from certain activities.**

MOST DANGEROUS	
riding a bicycle	1,000 to 1
boxing	14,000 to 1
horse racing	20,000 to 1
motor racing	30,000 to 1
skiing	1,000,000 to 1
LEAST DANGEROUS	

What do you think are the risks of dying from the activities below?

flying
riding a motorbike
living near a nuclear power station
driving a car
staying at home
smoking

2 **Read the text and find out the risks. Compare the results with your own ideas.**

If the government wanted to build a nuclear power station at the end of your street, what would you think? You would probably protest about it. But in fact, living next to a nuclear power station is less dangerous than driving a car and much safer than riding a motorbike or smoking.

Everything carries a risk — even walking down the street or staying at home. (There is a 100,000 to 1 risk of dying in an accident at home.) Why do people object to some risks but accept other much higher risks?

DAN

One reason is publicity. When an aeroplane crashes, a lot of people are killed at the same time. A plane crash is big news. A car crash is not. But travelling by road is far more dangerous than travelling by air. 1985 was the world's worst year for air disasters: over 2,000 people were killed. But in Britain alone, 5,000 people die in road accidents every year. (And Britain's roads are among the safest in the world.) The risks of dying in a plane crash are 25,000 to 1. Car drivers, however, run a risk of 11,000 to 1 and motorcyclists a horrific 500 to 1. In spite of this, fear of flying is much more common than fear of travelling by car.

A second reason is choice. If we choose to do something dangerous, we accept the risk. But we don't like it when someone else chooses it for us. We accept risks because we get some benefit from the activity. We accept the risks of driving a car or playing sports, because they make our lives more interesting. But, of course, people don't always choose safe things. People choose to smoke when smoking twenty cigarettes a day carries a 200 to 1 risk of death from heart disease and lung cancer.

A third reason is age. Over seventy per cent of all motorcycle accidents involve young men between 16 and 25. Every summer millions of young people risk skin cancer from sunbathing because they want to look healthier or more beautiful.

So how do you feel now about the nuclear power station and its risk of several million to 1? Would you still protest?

GER

3 **Answer these questions.**

a People accept some risks, but not others. The author gives three reasons. What are they?
b What examples does he give for each reason?
c What point is the author making about nuclear power stations?

WORD WORK

4 **Find all the words in the text connected with transport.**

5 **What do you think? Why do people run these unnecessary risks?**

FOLLOW UP

6 **Read through the text again. Underline any unknown words and look them up in a dictionary.**

LISTENING

At the doctor's

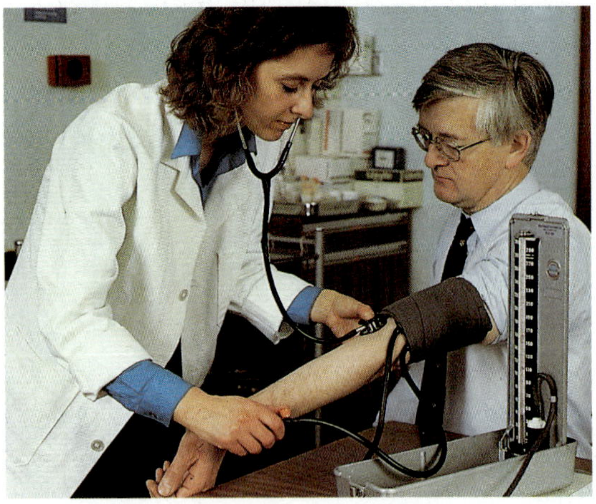

1 Some patients are at the doctor's.

a Look at this list of illnesses. Use a dictionary. Find out what they mean.

a broken arm	a rash	a cold
a sore throat	toothache	a temperature
earache	flu	a headache
a sprained ankle	a cough	

b Listen. What is wrong with the patients?

2 Listen again and complete the chart for each patient.

Patient	Problem	Diagnosis	Treatment
1			
2			

3 Which of these did the doctor mention?

FOLLOW UP

4 Complete the dialogue.

Patient Good ...., Doctor.

Doctor Good morning, what .... I do for you?

Patient I don't .... very well. I've got a .... and a ....

Doctor Hmm. Let me .... a look. Open your ...., please. Say aah.

Patient Aaah

Doctor Your .... a bit red. Is it ....?

Patient Yes. I feel all .... and cold, too.

Doctor I'll just .... your temperature. Can you put this under your .... Hmm, a hundred and one. Yes, you've got a ....

Patient What is it, then, Doctor?

Doctor You've got .... I'll give you a .... for some .... Take one spoonful every four ....

Patient Should I .... in bed?

Doctor No, but you .... stay at home and keep warm. Come back .... a week.

Patient Thank you, Doctor. Goodbye.

Doctor Goodbye.

INTERACTION

Describing illness

1 Put this conversation in the correct order.

Patient Yesterday. I fell over while I was playing football.

Patient Should I go today?

Doctor Goodbye.

Doctor Hmm. I think you've only sprained it. But you'll need an X-ray. I'll put a bandage on it for now. But you should go to hospital for an X-ray.

Patient Yes, but it hurts.

Patient I've hurt my ankle.

Patient Thank you, Doctor. Goodbye.

Doctor Can you just take your shoe off? Hmm, yes. Can you move your foot?

Doctor Yes. Take this letter with you.

Doctor When did it happen?

Doctor Hello. What's the problem?

2 Listen and check your order.

3 Complete these expressions.

I'..................	a headache. toothache. a sore throat. a temperature. flu. earache. stomach ache. a rash. a cold.

I've ....my	ankle. leg. arm. hand. face. foot.

My	leg eye ear arm knee	....

4 Look at these people.

a What will they tell the doctor? What will the doctor say they should do?

b Work in pairs. One person is the patient and one is the doctor. Make their conversations.

FOLLOW UP

5 Make Sue's conversation with the doctor.

PROJECT

How dangerous is your life?

We do many things in our life even when we know they are dangerous.

a Make a list of things that you do in your life that could be dangerous.

b Which things do you think are the most dangerous and the least dangerous? Make a chart like the one below.

c Write about the dangerous things that you do. Explain why you do them and what benefit you get from taking the risk.

d Compare your life to other people in the class. Is your life more or less dangerous than your friends'?

windsurfing

sunbathing

hitch-hiking

skiing

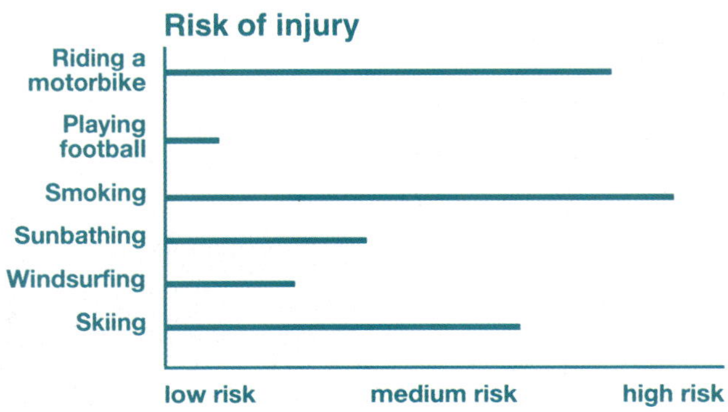

riding a motorbike without a helmet

Learning diary 6

1 What have you learnt in this unit? Look at the first page of the unit. How well have you achieved the learning objectives?

2 Do the self-check in the Workbook.

3 Look at the topics in units 1 to 6. Which topics did you like best? Write down your three favourite topics. Why did you like them? Discuss your answers with other members of your class.

▶ **Pronunciation: page 113**

7 coping

relative clauses/pronouns

Contents

Learning objectives

In this unit you will learn how to:

- describe people
- describe things
- understand descriptions
- find out information from a catalogue
- describe the features of something
- describe something that you don't know the name of
- find out what something is called
- cope with new situations in a foreign country

Preview task

In this unit Carmen comes to Victoria Road. She has never been to England before. What problems do you think she will have:

- with the culture?
- with the language?

Carmen arrives

1 What do you remember? What happened in the last part of the story? Look back at page 54 and check your ideas.

2 Look at this episode. Who are the people? Where are they? What are they doing?

3 Listen and follow in your books.

Carmen Excuse me. Can you tell me where … er … how I get to Victoria Road, please?

Terry Yes, I live there.

Carmen Oh, do you know Sue Scott?

Terry Yes, I live next door to her. I'm Terry.

Carmen Are you the boy who … er … that is going out with Sue? Yes I recognize you now. You were in a photograph that Sue send to … er … that Sue sent me.

Terry Yes, that's right. But I'm not going out with her any more. She's going out with a guy that she met at a dance.

Carmen Oh, I'm sorry … I …

Terry So, you must be Carmen. But what are you doing here on your own?

Carmen Sue was not at the airport. I wait for ... no, I waited for an hour and I called the telephone number which Sue gave me. But nobody ... er ... you know ...

Terry There was no reply.

Carmen Yes, there was no reply. So I came with the train.

Terry You came by train. That was very brave. Well come on. I'll take your suitcase.

Outside Sue's house

Terry You're right. There's nobody in. I wonder what's up. You can wait at my place till someone comes.

At Terry's house

Carmen Oh, is this the girl which ... no ... er the girl who go to America? I'm sorry. My English is very bad. Please correct me. I want to learn.

Terry You speak very good English. Yes, that's Jackie, the girl who went to America, or you can say 'the girl that went to America', but not 'the girl which went ...'. Good lord! An ambulance has just stopped outside Sue's house.

In the street

Carmen Oh, Sue. What has happened to you?

Sue Carmen. Thank God you're all right. But I'm so sorry, Carmen. The doctor says I've got to stay in bed for two weeks.

Terry Don't worry, Sue. I'll look after Carmen.

4 Answer these questions.

- **a** Where did Carmen meet Terry?
- **b** How did she recognize him?
- **c** How long did Carmen wait at the airport?
- **d** What happened when she telephoned Sue?
- **e** How did she get to Hartfield?
- **f** What did Carmen and Terry do at his house?
- **g** What did Carmen say about her English?
- **h** How did Sue arrive home?
- **i** What has happened to Sue?
- **j** What must Sue do?

5 Close your book. Listen to the dialogue again.

Useful expressions

6 **How do you say these in your language?**

Can you tell me how I get to ...?

I live next door to ...

She's going out with ...

What are you doing here?

on your own

There was no reply.

There's nobody in.

I wonder what's up.

at my place

Good lord!

Thank God you're all right.

I'll look after ...

7 **Work in groups of three. Each person takes one of the parts.**

a Read the dialogue.

b Change roles and read the dialogue again.

FOLLOW UP

8 **Terry is telling Sue's mother about Carmen. Complete what they say.**

Mrs Scott How did Carmen get to Hartfield?

Terry Well, she .... at the .... for an .... and then she took the .... to Hartfield.

Mrs Scott Why didn't she .... ?

Terry She did. She .... the number that Sue gave ...., but there was no ....

Mrs Scott Oh yes, there was .... in. We were at the ....

Terry I know. When .... got here there was still nobody .... So we waited .... my place. We .... looking at some ...., when the .... arrived.

LANGUAGE WORK

Relative clauses

1 **Look at this sentence.**

You were in a photo	that Sue sent me.
We call this **the main clause.**	We call this **the relative clause.**

a Find more examples of sentences with relative clauses in the story.

b Underline the relative clauses.

2 **Look at the picture. Carmen is describing the people. What does she say?**

Example
Sue is the girl that has got a broken arm.

Relative pronouns

3 **Look at this.**

That's Jackie, the girl who went to America, or you can say 'the girl that went to America', but not 'the girl which went to America'.

a What is the rule for using '**who**' and '**which**'?

b Look at these sentences. Check your rule.

I called the number which Sue gave me.
I called the number that Sue gave me.

Are you the boy who lives next door?
Are you the boy that lives next door?

This is the ambulance which brought Sue home.
This is the ambulance that brought Sue home.

Joe is the guy who Sue met at a dance.
Joe is the guy that Sue met at a dance.

c Complete the rule for relative pronouns with these words.

things people

We use 'who' for ______________.
We use 'which' for ______________.
We use 'that' for ______________.

4 **What kinds of things annoy you?**

people who drop litter in the street

people that are late

telephones that are out of order

machines which are empty

a Write down examples of people and things that annoy you.

b Go round the class and ask people: 'What annoys you?'

c Make a list of the things that annoy people in your class.

FOLLOW UP

5 **Write the answers to Exercise 2.**

READING

Watches

1 Look at these watches.

a Which do you think is the most expensive?

b Which one would you choose?

2 Read these descriptions. Write the catalogue numbers next to the correct watch. Some of the watches have the same catalogue number.

3 How did you match the texts to the pictures? What clues did you use?

1 cat. no.

LCD Digital / Calculator Watch

Black resin case and strap, digital 12 hour display, day and alarm functions. Features full calculator functions,world time and telememo. Guaranteed one year.

Special Offer!

Maker's Recommended Price £36.99

Our Price £24.99. ***Save*** £12.00

20H072 £24.99

Dual Display Analogue / Digital Watch

White dial, electronic setting, analogue movement and digital display of hours/ minutes/seconds/day.Stainless steel case and bracelet. Water resistant. Guaranteed one year.

Special Offer!

Maker's Recommended Price £25.95

Our Price £15.95. ***Save*** £10.00

20H109 £15.95

Watches

2 cat. no.

3 cat. no.

Gold Plated Analogue/Digital Watch

Analogue dial plus digital display of hours/minutes/seconds/day/date. With 24 hour alarm and hourly chime. Water resistant. Available with round or square face. Guaranteed one year.

Special Offer!

Maker's Recommended Price

square face £25.99, *round face* £30.99

Our Price *square face* £17.99, *round face* £22.99. ***Save*** £8.00

square 20K014 £17.99

round 20K022 £22.99

5 cat. no.

Quartz Analogue Watch

Traditional round white dial with roman numerals. Hour, minute and second hands. Gold plated case and leather strap. Water resistant. Guaranteed one year.

11K178 £40.75

Also available with day, date and 24-hour display.

11K184 £44.90

Plastic Quartz Analogue Watch (Pop Swatch)

Water resistant to 30m. Elasticated fabric strap. Available in a variety of patterns and colours. Guaranteed one year.

Special Offer!

Maker's Recommended Price £28.50

Our Price £23.50. ***Save*** £5.00

20PS101 £23.50

4 cat. no.

6 cat. no.

7 cat. no.

8 cat. no.

Sports Quartz Analogue / Digital Watch

Black resin case and strap. Analogue movement with luminous hands and digital display of time/day/date. Features full memory stopwatch up to 100 laps and countdown alarm accurate to 1/100th second. Three daily alarms, hourly chime. Water resistant. Guaranteed one year.
20H164 £29.95

9 cat. no.

Quartz Analogue / Alarm Watch

Diver's watch with black dial, luminous hands and markings. Chrome plated case with black rubber strap. Shock resistant and water resistant. Guaranteed one year.
Special Offer!
Maker's Recommended Price £59.99
Our Price £49.99. ***Save*** £10.00
20H155 £49.99

11 cat. no.

10 cat. no.

4 **Read the descriptions again.**

a Complete this chart with information about each watch.

catalogue number	display (analogue/ digital)	material	time functions	special functions/ features	MRP	price

b Look at your chart. How many watches:

- have got a bracelet?
- have got a strap?
- have got an alarm?
- are water resistant?
- are shock resistant?
- are gold or chrome plated?
- are on special offer?

WORD WORK

5 **Look at the pictures again.**

a Label one example of each of these.

a strap
a case
a bracelet
a dial
a digital display
a second hand
a minute hand
an hour hand
an analogue display
a face

b How did you work out the meanings of these words?

6 **What kind of person would buy each watch? Why?**

7 **Work in a group. Make a catalogue of the watches people in your class have.**

FOLLOW UP

8 **Describe the ideal watch.**

LISTENING

What do you call it?

In a foreign language you don't always know the correct word for something. What can you do?

1 **Look at the pictures.**

a Do you know the names of the things?

b Choose one of the things. You are in Britain and you want to talk about it. What can you do, if you don't know the name?

Example
You can describe its shape.

2 **Look at the pictures and listen. What are the English words that Carmen is looking for?**

3 **Listen again. How many of the things can you name?**

4 **Listen again.**

a How does Carmen say what she wants?

Example
She describes its colour.

b Compare your answers to your ideas from Exercise 1b.

FOLLOW UP

5 **Use a dictionary. Match these names to the correct pictures.**

socket pillow cushion button
plug shoelaces buckle zip

INTERACTION

Describing things

1 Match these descriptions to objects in the pictures.

electrical	human	tall
colourful	plastic	round
sticky	soft	flat
long and thin	metal	
black and white	pointed	

2 Work in pairs. One person chooses an object and describes it. The other person must guess what it is.

It's . . . . It has got . . . .

3 Match these descriptions to the correct pictures.

a It's something that you use for cooking.
b It's something which you find in the kitchen.
c It's a bird that can't fly.
d It's a bird which lives in Africa.
e It's someone who sells things.
f It's a person that works in a shop.

4 Practise describing things.

a Write these things on a piece of paper.

- the name of something that you need to buy
- an animal
- a job

b Fold the piece of paper and give it to another person in the class.

c Work in pairs. Look at the paper that you have received but don't show it to your partner. You must describe the things to your partner without using the names. He/she must try to guess what you want to say.

Example
The thing that I need to buy is something that you drink. You drink it with meals. It's a drink which can be red or white.

d Change roles. The other person must now describe the things on his/her paper.

FOLLOW UP

5 Look at the things on your piece of paper. Write descriptions of them.

PROJECT

Culture shock

1 **You are going to another country. What would you worry about doing? Work in groups and make a list of things.**

2 **Some English-speaking visitors are coming to your country.**

a Look at the list that you made in Exercise 1. Choose some of the situations.

b Write a guide for your visitors.

- Describe what they have to do.
- Give some useful words and expressions with translations.

understanding a railway timetable

finding your way round the town

buying a train ticket

understanding a menu

using a different currency

using a public telephone

▶ **Pronunciation: page 113**

Learning diary

7

1. What have you learnt in this unit? Look at the first page of the unit. How well have you achieved the learning objectives?
2. Do the self-check in the Workbook.
3. Look at what Carmen says:

How do you feel when you are corrected?

Does it help you to learn?

How do you like to be corrected?

Discuss your answers with other members of your class.

READING

1 Look quickly at the text.

a What is it about?

- the risks that sports stars take
- advertising sports
- the money that sports stars earn
- drugs that are used in sport

b What is a sponsor?

- someone who earns a lot of money from playing sport
- someone who pays sports stars to advertise a product
- a sports star who takes drugs
- a sports star who advertises things

Sports Profile

When the athlete, Ben Johnson, was disqualified from the Seoul Olympic games for taking drugs, he lost more than his gold medal and his good name. He said goodbye to $5 million in possible sponsorship money. Sport is big business. Today's sports stars can earn as much on television as they can on the tennis court, golf course or football pitch.

Most of the money comes from advertising clothes, sports equipment, drinks and other products. Ivan Lendl earns £1.3 million a year for wearing Adidas clothes and Ray-Ban sunglasses. He is the world's richest tennis player. The richest sports star of all is the boxer, Muhammed Ali. He has earned £39 million in and out of the boxing ring. Most of the money in boxing comes from prize money. Sponsors like sports which have a cleaner, more glamorous image than boxing — sports like tennis, golf, motor racing and skiing.

Sports can change their image. At one time snooker was only a game that was played in clubs. But since colour television arrived, it has become the most popular sport on British television. Top snooker player, Steve Davis, earns over £1 million a year in prize money, sponsorship and fees for appearing on television. On the other hand, some sports, like athletics and football, are less popular with sponsors because of bad publicity about drugs and fighting by fans.

Sponsors want the best image for their products. They want stars who are the best on the athletics track or the motor racing circuit. But they also want stars who are good-looking and who have an interesting personality - stars like Argentina's young tennis player, Gabriela Sabatini, Spanish golfer, Severano Ballesteros, French motor racing driver, Alain Prost, America's running star, 'Flo Jo' Johnson or Switzerland's champion skier, Pirmin Zubriggen.

2 Right, Wrong or Don't know?

	✓	✖	?
a Ben Johnson was disqualified for taking drugs.	❑	❑	❑
b The gold medal was taken away from him.	❑	❑	❑
c Ben Johnson earns $5 million a year.	❑	❑	❑
d Sports stars earn more money from prize money than from sponsorship.	❑	❑	❑
e Muhammed Ali has earned more than any other sports star.	❑	❑	❑
f Sponsors think that skiing is a glamorous sport.	❑	❑	❑
g Snooker is the most popular sport in Britain	❑	❑	❑
h Sponsors are worried about footballers who fight.	❑	❑	❑
i Alain Prost advertises cars.	❑	❑	❑

3 Sports and players

a Label these sports.

b Find the names of people in the text connected with each sport.

c Say what each person is.

Example
Ivan Lendl is a tennis player.

4 Complete these sentences with the verbs in brackets.

a Ben Johnson .... from the Seoul Olympics. (disqualify)

b Ivan Lendl .... by Adidas. (sponsor)

c Football's image .... by fighting among fans. (damage)

d Drugs .... by some sports stars. (take)

e Many different products .... by sports stars. (advertise)

f £39 million .... by Muhammed Ali. (earn)

g Snooker's image .... by colour TV. (change)

h In Britain, Snooker .... by more people than any other sport. (watch)

i Boxing .... by many sponsors. (not like)

j Good-looking sports stars .... by sponsors. (want)

5 What do you think?

a Imagine that you produce clothes. Who would you sponsor to wear them? Why?

b Some people think that cigarettes and drinks should not be advertised through sport. Do you agree? Are there any other products that sports stars should not advertise?

FOLLOW UP

6 Who advertises what? Watch television and look at magazines. Find out what products sports stars advertise. Write about them.

Example
Adidas sports products are advertised by Ivan Lendl.

LISTENING

Free time

1 You are going to hear part of a radio programme. First read this.

DJ According to a national survey, Britain's kids spend most of their free time watching television. We went to a local school and talked to a group of 16- and 17-year-old pupils. What do young people do in their free time?

2 What do you think the most common activities are?

a Work in groups. Choose the top five.

b Do you think it is the same for boys and girls?

c Compare your list to other groups.

3 Listen. Which activities are mentioned?

helping with housework
shopping
eating
listening to the radio
talking on the telephone
doing community work
listening to records
watching sport
window shopping
working in a part-time job
playing a musical instrument
going to the cinema
doing nothing
babysitting
going to the hairdresser's
talking to friends
putting on makeup
playing a sport

4 Listen again. Which activities do young people spend most time on?

a Draw a chart like the one below.

b List the top five activities for the boys and girls.

c Compare this list to the one you worked out.

girls	boys

WORD WORK

5 Activities

a Name:

- two kinds of sport that you do in water;
- two kinds of housework that teenagers do;
- two kinds of jobs that teenagers do.

b Listen again and check your answers.

FOLLOW UP

6 How do young people in your country spend their time?

a Work in pairs. Decide what you think are the top five activities.

b Work in groups. Report what you have discussed. Make a list of the activities discussed by the whole group.

c Write about your list.

- How many different activities do you have on your list?
- Are there some activities that are more popular with the boys or girls?
- What is the most popular thing?
- Is it the most popular for everyone in the group?

d Compare your list to the one in Exercise 4. What differences are there?

GOING FOR GOLD

► Pronunciation: page 113

9 up, up and away

modal verbs

Contents

Learning objectives

In this unit you will learn how to:

- express wishes
- express ability
- describe a route
- express polite instructions
- check in at an airport
- respond to unexpected information

Preview task

In this unit you will learn about two modal verbs. These are important verbs, but you can only use them in certain tenses. Look through the unit.

- What are the two verbs?
- What must you use for the other tenses?

Find some examples in the Victoria Road story.

Carmen's discovery

1 **What do you remember? What happened in the last part of the story? Look back at page 64 and check your ideas.**

2 **Look at this episode. Who are the people? Where are they? What are they doing? Why is Carmen surprised?**

3 **Listen and follow in your books.**

Sue I feel so angry with myself. I haven't been able to take you to places. And now you've only got three days left.

Carmen Yes, the time has gone very quickly. I wish I could stay longer.

Sue Oh, could you stay longer, Carmen? That would be wonderful. I'll be able to go out next week. Oh, please stay, Carmen.

Vince Will you be able to change your ticket?

Carmen I don't know. I'll have to go to a travel . . . er . . . shop?

Vince I've got a friend who works in a travel agency. I'll take you tomorrow.

The next day

Agent Can I help you? Oh hi, Vince.

Vince Hi, Kim. Is it possible to change the return flight on this ticket?

Later

Vince I'm sorry, Carmen. I couldn't change it. It would cost an extra £200. It's a special fare, you see, and you can't change the return flight. You'll have to go back on Monday after all.

Carmen So I won't be able to stay longer. That's a pity. Sue will be very disappointed.

Carmen Vince, can you see that guy over there? Is that Joe?

Vince Oh, yes it is. Haven't you met Super Joe yet?

Carmen Super? Oh, I see. No. I've seen his photograph. But he hasn't been to see Sue since the accident.

Vince I know. Anyway, I must be off. See you later, Carmen.

A few moments later

Carmen Oh, who's that girl? . . . And what's this? The Kingman Property Company!

What do you think?

- What should Carmen do?
- What would you do, if you were her?

4 Answer these questions.

a How much longer is Carmen staying?
b Why is Sue angry with herself?
c Why does Sue want Carmen to stay longer?
d Does Carmen want to stay longer?
e Where will Carmen have to go to change the ticket?
f Why couldn't Vince change the ticket?
g What won't Carmen be able to do?
h How does Carmen recognize Joe?
k What happens when Vince leaves?
l Where do Joe and the girl go?

5 Close your book. Listen to the dialogue again.

Useful expressions

6 **How do you say these in your language?**

I feel so angry with myself.

I wish I could . . .

Is it possible to . . .?

That's a pity.

She'll be very disappointed.

that guy over there

I must be off.

7 **Work in groups of four. Each person takes one of the parts. Read the dialogue.**

FOLLOW UP

8 **Carmen is talking to Terry. Complete their conversation.**

Terry Hello, Carmen. .... wrong?

Carmen I'm worried .... Sue.

Terry Why?

Carmen Well, Sue wants me to stay .... So I tried to .... the return flight on my .... I went to a travel .... with Vince yesterday, but I .... change it.

Terry Are .... worried because Sue will be .... ?

Carmen No. You see, when we .... out of the travel agency, we .... Joe. Vince calls him .... Joe, you know. Anyway, I .... him from a photo that Sue .... got.

Terry Oh, I see.

Carmen Well, ... was with a girl. They .... holding hands.

Terry What .... you do?

Carmen I followed .... They went into an .... — the King Property .... or something like that.

Terry The .... Property Company?

Carmen Yes, ... right. But now I .... know what to do.

LANGUAGE WORK

Expressing wishes

1 **Complete the expression.**

I wish I .... stay longer.

2 **What do you wish you could do or be? Write down three things.**

3 **What do these people wish they could do?**

'can' or 'be able to'

4 Look at these sentences.

I can go out with Carmen.
I can't go out with Carmen.

a Change the sentences using these expressions.

Yesterday . . .
Since my accident . . .
Tomorrow . . .

b Use your sentences to complete this rule.

> **'Can' has got a past form: ________ but it hasn't got a form for the present perfect or the ________. For these tenses we must use the verb ________.**

5 What hasn't Sue been able to do since her accident? Look at this list. Say what Sue has or hasn't been able to do.

Example
She has been able to eat.
She hasn't been able to go out.

eat	write letters	have driving lessons
go out	have a bath	work at the hospital
read	go swimming	go for a walk
wash up	ride a bicycle	go to the cinema
watch TV	visit friends	play badminton

**6 Next week Sue's leg will be all right, but her arm will still be strapped up.
Work in pairs. Sue is talking to the doctor. She is asking what she will be able to do. Make their conversation.**

Example
A *'Will I be able to go out?'*
B *'Yes, you will.'*
A *'Will I be able to ride a bicycle?'*
B *'No, you won't.'*

FOLLOW UP

7 What has Carmen been able to do that she can't do at home? What hasn't she been able to do? Write six things for each.

Example
She has been able to hear a lot of English.
She hasn't been able to speak Spanish.

READING

1 **Look at the magazine page opposite. What is it about?**

2 **Read these questions.**

- Who is running the competition?
- What will the winners get?
- What must you do?
- What information about yourself must you give?
- What is the closing date for entries?
- Where must you send the entry form to?

a Now look quickly at the text. Find the place where you think you will find the information. It is not necessary to understand everything.

b Look at those parts again and find the answers.

3 **Show the prize winners' route on the map.**

a Mark the places that they will visit.

b Show how they will travel between each place.

4 **Run the competition in your class.**

a Copy the entry form.

b Complete it.

c Put all the entry forms in a box or bag.

d Find the winners.

5 **Look back at the text. Which parts didn't you read? Did you need to?**

WORD WORK

6 **Make a word tree. Find as many words as possible in the text to add to the tree.**

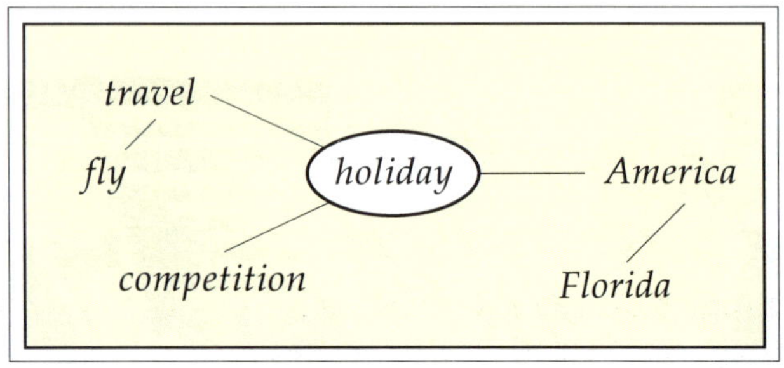

FOLLOW UP

7 **You are one of the prize winners. Describe what you did on your holiday.**

We flew by British Airways Concorde to New York. We spent two days in the Big Apple and then we . . .

WIN WIN WIN

in our great holiday competition

1st prize a fly-drive holiday for two in the USA

2nd prize a weekend for two in New York

3rd prize £500 worth of Western Jeans products

Disney World, the Golden Gate Bridge, the Statue of Liberty — all the places you have dreamed about. Now this can be yours in our holiday-of-a-lifetime competition. Our prize winners will fly by British Airways Concorde to New York. You'll spend two days in the Big Apple and then you'll pick up your Cadillac and drive down the east coast to Washington DC and then on to the Deep South: Florida, Alabama, Mississippi, Texas. You'll be able to visit Walt Disney World, then the Space Centre at Cape Canaveral and the famous cities of New Orleans and Dallas. From Dallas you'll travel by plane to the west coast. Here you'll visit San Francisco, Los Angeles and Hollywood. Finally you'll fly back to New York for the flight home. You'll stay in the best hotels and we'll give you £500 each to spend.

Can you believe it? Three weeks in the Good Old USA? Just answer the six simple questions, fill in your name and address and post it to arrive not later than 18th October.

This is what you do

1 Here are some questions about cities in the United States. The names are all in the text. Find the answers and write the names next to the correct numbers in the coupon below.

   1 Which Californian city was destroyed by an earthquake in 1906?

   2 Which city is at the mouth of the Mississippi River?

   3 What is the capital of the USA?

   4 Of which city is Hollywood a suburb?

   5 Which is the largest city in the USA?

   6 Which American city is famous for oil?

2 Fill in your name and address and post your entry to the address below.

Western Jeans competition
EG Publicity
Slough
SL9 5DF

Closing date: 18th October

HOLIDAY COMPETITION

Answers

1 ______________ *4* ______________

2 ______________ *5* ______________

3 ______________ *6* ______________

Name ______________________________

Address ______________________________

Rules: The competition is open only to UK residents aged 18 and over, excluding employees of Western Jeans (UK) Ltd. The first prize will be awarded to the first correct entry drawn after 18th October. The second and third prizes will be awarded to the next two correct entries drawn. Prizes are as stated. No cash alternatives. The judges' decision will be final. No correspondence will be entered into. The names of the winners will be published.

LISTENING

Check-in

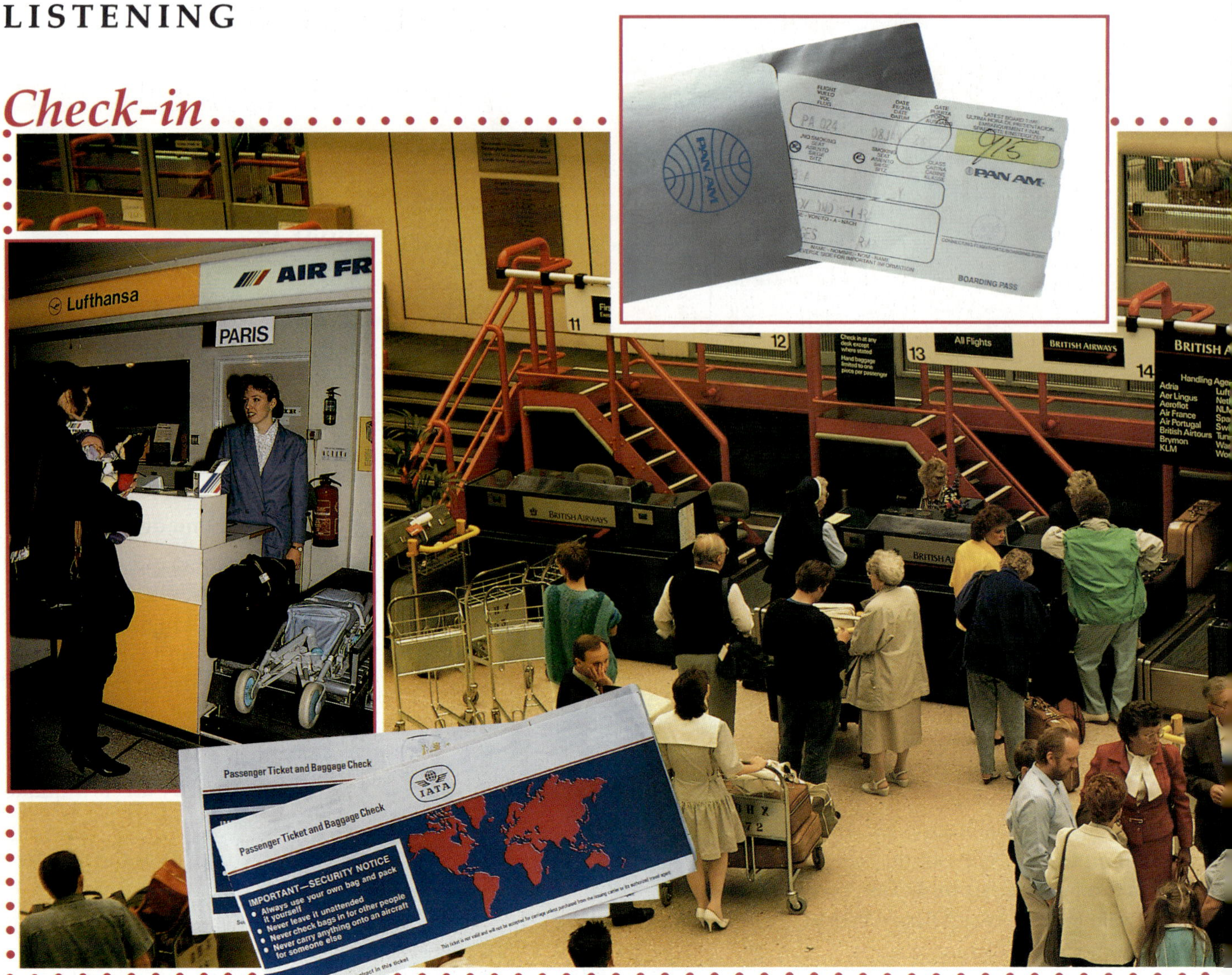

1 **Look at the following conversation. Number the parts in the correct order.**

- [ ] Here's a label for your hand baggage. Do you want smoking or non-smoking?
- [ ] Here's your boarding card. Boarding will be at 10.45 at departure gate number 22. Have a nice flight.
- [ ] Yes. Can I have your ticket and your passport, please?
- [ ] I'm sorry. All the window seats are taken. Do you want an aisle seat?
- [ ] Just that one. This one is hand baggage.
- [1] Hello. Do I check in here for Miami?
- [ ] Thank you. How many pieces of baggage are you checking in?
- [ ] Yes, all right.
- [ ] Thank you.
- [ ] Here you are.
- [ ] Non-smoking, please. I'd like a window seat, if you've got one.

2 **Listen and check your order.**

3 **Work in pairs. Act the dialogue with your partner.**

4 **Role play the dialogue with this information.**

a **flight to Athens:** hand baggage only; smoking; boarding 14:25; gate 7

b **flight to Sao Paulo:** two suitcases; non-smoking; boarding 9:50; gate 15

* At a travel agency

Customer: Excuse me. How long is the flight from London to New York?
Assistant: Just a minute, sir.
Customer: Good lord. That's fast.

WORD WORK

5 Look at the pictures.

a Label these things.

check-in desk	suitcase
check-in clerk	hand baggage
passenger	label
boarding card	ticket
passport	departure gate

b Find another word for 'luggage'.

FOLLOW UP

6 You are going on holiday. Write your dialogue at the check-in desk at the airport. Use the dialogue in Exercise 2 to help you.

INTERACTION

'must' and 'have to'

1 Look at the Victoria Road story on page 78.

a Complete the sentences.

I' .... go to a travel agency.

You' .... go back on Monday after all.

b What word does **'have to'** replace in these sentences?

did can must should

c Complete this rule.

> 'Must' has only got a __________ tense. For other tenses, we use the verb 'to ________ to'.

2 Some people are checking in at the airport. Look at the check-in clerk's statements. What will the people have to do?

Example
I'm sorry. You're too early.
They'll have to wait.

I'm sorry. Today's flight has been cancelled.
I'm sorry. You can't check in for that flight at this desk.
I'm sorry. Your luggage is 10 kilos overweight.
I'm sorry. Your ticket is not valid for this flight.
I'm sorry. You're only allowed to take one piece of hand baggage on board.
I'm sorry. You haven't got a visa for the United States. You won't be allowed on the plane.
I'm sorry. I haven't got any seats in the non-smoking section.
You're very late. The flight leaves in fifteen minutes.

3 Conversations sometimes take unexpected turns. Look at the dialogue at the check-in counter on page 84. Then read the check-in clerk's statements in Exercise 2 above again.

a When would the clerk say these things in the dialogue?

b What would the passenger say?

c Make new dialogues.

FOLLOW UP

4 Write two of your dialogues from Exercise 3c.

PROJECT

Your own competition

1 **Work in groups. Decide:**

- Who is running the competition?
- What will the prizes be?
- What must the people do?

2 **Write the text for your competition. (You needn't write the rules. You can use the rules on page 83.)**

3 **Illustrate your competition.**

4 **Run the competition in your class.**

Holiday time

Verse 1

Summer is _____ and the weather is _____ .
I've got _____ on my mind.
_____ on now. Don't be _____ .
My bags _____ packed and I'm _____ to go.

Chorus

Cos, it's _____ time, holiday time.
Come _____ now. It's holiday time.
Holiday _____, holiday time.
Come on now. _____ holiday time.

Verse 2

Well, I'm _____ in the _____ at a quarter to _____.
The taxi's _____ and I _____ be late.
Tickets and _____ in my hand.
I'm off to the _____ and the _____ and the _____.

Verse 3

Hey, Mister _____, in your _____ grey bird.
Take _____ to the _____ side of the _____ .
East or _____. I _____ care.
Take me to the _____ . Take me _____ .

► **Pronunciation: page 114**

Learning diary

9

1 What have you learnt in this unit? Look at the first page of the unit. How well have you achieved the learning objectives?

2 Do the self-check in the Workbook.

3 In this unit you have learnt about an irregular part of the English language. Irregular forms are found in all languages. Think of some examples where your language is irregular. What problems do you think learners of your language have? Do you have these problems in learning English irregular forms? Discuss your answers with other members of your class.

10 problems

going to; modal verbs

Contents

Learning objectives

In this unit you will learn how to:

- express intentions
- give or refuse permission
- state rules and restrictions
- describe a problem
- give advice
- describe conditions in the past

Preview task

In this unit you will learn a new way of talking about the future.

- Look through the unit and find it.
- Find examples of it in the Victoria Road story.

Sue runs away

1 What do you remember? What happened in the last part of the story? Look back at page 78 and check your ideas.

2 Look at this episode. Who are the people? Why is Sue upset? Why does Mrs Scott shout, 'John, John!'?

3 Listen and follow in your books.

Mr Scott And I said 'No'. You aren't going to see that Joe again. He's caused enough trouble in this house.

Sue You treat me like a child. I'm 17 years old and I'm not allowed to do anything.

Mrs Scott That's not fair, Susan. You're allowed to do lots of things.

Sue I'm only allowed to do what you want.

Mr Scott Sue. Come back here.

Mrs Scott Oh leave her alone, dear. She'll get over it.

Later

Kamala Great news, Sue! They aren't going to cut down the trees. We've won.

Sue Oh, I don't care any more.

Kamala But you were so interested before!

Sue Well, everything is going to be different from now on, Kam.

Kamala What do you mean, Sue? What are you going to do?

Sue All my life I've been a good little girl. I've always done my homework. I've worked at the hospital. I've helped to save the trees.

Kamala But what's wrong with that, Sue? You've always been very sensible.

Sue I'm fed up with being sensible and I'm not going to be sensible any more. I'm going to leave school and get a job. First I'm going to dye my hair green. From now on I'm going to do just what I want. You'll see.

Next day

Mrs Scott John, John!

Mr Scott Wha . . . Ow!

Mr Scott Oh, my head. What on earth is the matter?

Mrs Scott Never mind your head. It's Sue. Her bedroom's empty and her suitcase isn't there. She's gone!

What do you think?

- Where has Sue gone?
- What is she going to do?

4 Right, Wrong or Don't know?

		✓	✖	?
a	Sue and her parents are arguing about Joe.	❑	❑	❑
b	Sue's mother agrees with her father.	❑	❑	❑
c	Kamala is 17 years old.	❑	❑	❑
d	Sue isn't allowed to have a boyfriend.	❑	❑	❑
e	The Kingman Property Company aren't going to cut down the trees.	❑	❑	❑
f	Sue is very happy about the news.	❑	❑	❑
g	Sue isn't going to work at the hospital any more.	❑	❑	❑
h	Kamala is going to dye her hair red.	❑	❑	❑
i	Kamala thinks Sue is very sensible.	❑	❑	❑
j	Sue has taken some clothes with her.	❑	❑	❑
k	Sue is going to run away with Joe.	❑	❑	❑

5 Close your book. Listen to the dialogue again.

Useful expressions

6 How do you say these in your language?

to cause trouble	
You treat me like a child.	
That's not fair.	
Leave her alone.	
She'll get over it.	
Great news!	
I don't care any more.	
a good little girl	
I'm fed up . . .	
with . . .ing . . .	
I'm going to do just what I want.	
What on earth is the matter?	
Never mind . . .	

7 Work in groups of four. Each person takes one of the parts. Read the dialogue.

FOLLOW UP

8 Sue left this letter for her parents. Complete it.

Dear ______ and Dad,

I'm ______ home. I'm ______ up with being treated like a ______. I'm 17 years ______ and I'm not ______ to do anything. I'm only allowed ______ do what you want. ______ always been a good ______ girl. I've worked ______ the hospital. I've helped ______ the housework and I've always ______ my homework. Well, I'm fed ______ with being ______. From now on I'm ______ to do just ______ I want. I'm going ______ leave school and I'm going to ______ a job.

Please ______ try to find me. I'm sorry.

love,

Sue

LANGUAGE WORK

going to

1 Use the Victoria Road story to help you.

a Complete this table.

I	am am not		leave home. run away.
He She It	.... is not 's isn't	going	see Joe. cut down the trees.
We You They	are are not 're		have a good time.

b Look at these two sentences.

I **will leave** school.
I **am going to leave** school.

These both show the future. But '**going to**' shows a definite future.

I will leave school (when I am old enough).

= It will happen at some time in the future.

I am going to leave school (next week).

= I have decided to leave school and it will definitely happen at a particular time.

2 New Year's resolutions

a These people are making New Year's resolutions. What are they going to do?

Example
Mrs Jones is going to stop smoking.

b Work in pairs. Ask about the people below.

Example
A *'What is Mrs Jones going to do?'*
B *'She's going to stop smoking.'*

Permission

3 Look at the Victoria Road story.

a Complete what Sue and her mother say.

You' .... to do lots of things.

I' .... to do anything.

b When are you allowed to do these things in your country?

Example
You are allowed to leave school when you are sixteen.

leave school	ride a motorbike
get married	join the army
drink alcohol	go to university
smoke	play slot machines
leave home	get a bank loan
drive a car	work part-time

c Change your answers like this.

You are not allowed to leave school till you are sixteen.

FOLLOW UP

4 Write ten things that you are not allowed to do at home or at school.

Two Limericks

There was a young man from Quebec
Who wrapped both his legs round his neck.
But the poor man forgot
How to untie the knot
And now he's an absolute wreck.

A lovely young lady from Gaul
Was asked to a fancy dress ball.
She thought she would risk it
And went as a biscuit
But the dog ate her up in the hall.

READING

1 **Here are some extracts from a magazine problem page. The parts are mixed up and two of the answers are missing. Match the titles, letters and answers.**

Write to Kate for advice on your problems

Advice

PROBLEMS WITH MUM

I've got a terrible problem. I've got a lot of spots on my face. My mum doesn't understand the problem. She says it's just acne and she says it's normal. But I don't want to go out because everyone laughs at me. What can I do?

Tim, Birmingham

Does he know how you feel about the problem? You must talk to him and explain that you want to be alone with him. Friends often feel jealous when their best friend starts going out with a boy or a girl. But Steve will have to choose between you and his friend. If he won't, then you have two choices: you can give him up and find another boyfriend, or you can bring your own best friend on dates, too.

BULLYING

I'm 16 and I've never had a boyfriend. But I'm not surprised. I'm fat, my hair's a mess and I haven't got any good clothes. My friends have all got boyfriends, but I'm so unattractive, I can't see how anyone could love me. It's not fair.

Jasmine, Liverpool

There's a gang of kids at our school who are making my life hell. A few weeks ago they asked me for money. I said No, but then they pushed me and hit me. Like a fool, I gave them my bus fare and so I had to walk home. But that was only the start of it. Every day after that they asked for more. I started taking money from my mum's purse to pay them. Now I can't face them any more. I haven't been to school for over a week. I'm so frightened. Please help me. I can't talk to anyone else about my problem.

Nicola, Edinburgh

NO BOYFRIEND

Your mother is right. Teenage acne is normal. It's part of growing up. Have a look at your schoolfriends. They've probably got spots, too. Use medicated products on your face and eat lots of fresh fruit and vegetables. If this doesn't help, go and see your doctor. He or she can prescribe a course of pills. But most of all, don't worry. Worrying only makes it worse.

THREE'S A CROWD

First of all, you must face the problem. Meeting in secret will only make the problem worse. Go and ask her mum why she doesn't like you. Perhaps she thinks that her daughter is too young to have a boyfriend. Most of all, you must show that you are sensible. If your girlfriend isn't allowed out after midnight, bring her home before 12.

SPOTS

My boyfriend, Steve, and I never go out on our own. He always brings his best friend with him, when we have a date. He says that he feels guilty if he doesn't invite his friend. But what about me?

Liz, Carlisle

My girlfriend and I love each other very much, but her mother doesn't like me at all. A couple of weeks ago, I took her home after midnight. There was a big argument and now I'm not allowed to go to her house any more. We have to meet in secret.

Robert, Bedford

2 **Fill in the names.**

a .... has got acne.

b ....'s girlfriend's mother doesn't like him.

c .... is afraid to go to school.

d ....'s boyfriend always brings his best friend on a date.

e .... had an argument with his girlfriend's mother.

f .... thinks that she's unattractive.

g .... has stolen money from her mother.

h .... has never had a boyfriend.

i .... wants to be alone with her boyfriend.

j .... feels jealous of her friends.

k .... brought his girlfriend home late.

l .... thinks that people laugh at him.

m .... meets his girlfriend in secret.

n .... has got a boyfriend called Steve.

3 **The letters that Kate receives are much longer than the letters that are printed. Which letters do you think these come from?**

Sharon is very upset about it, but I don't know what to do.

He's quite a nice guy and I don't want to hurt him.

Someone at school said my face looked like a pizza.

I never go out. I spend every evening watching television.

Last week I gave them some earrings that my grandmother gave me for Christmas. I had to say that I'd lost them.

WORD WORK

4 **Find all the words in the letters associated with 'relationships'.**

5 **What do you think?**

a Are these typical problems? Look in your magazines. What kinds of problems do young people write about?

b What do you think about the advice that is given?

6 **Two of the letters have no answers. What advice would you give? Choose one of them and write Kate's answer.**

FOLLOW UP

7 **Write Kate's answer to the other letter.**

Culture spot

Advice is often given in proverbs. Here are some English proverbs.

a What do you think they mean?

b Do you have similar proverbs in your language?

A bird in the hand is worth two in the bush.

Actions speak louder than words.

All that glitters is not gold.

Don't count your chickens until they are hatched.

Beauty is only skin deep.

Every cloud has a silver lining.

It's better to be safe than sorry.

Rome wasn't built in a day.

LISTENING

The good old days?

1 Read what the old man says.

a Have you heard it before?

b Do you agree?

2 Listen to the old man. What things does he talk about?

3 What are the good and bad things that the old man talks about?

a Make a chart like the one below.

bad things	reason
good things	**reason**

b Listen again and complete your chart.

'must' and 'can'

4 What does the old man say?

a Put these two sentences into the past and complete what he says.

I must walk to school.
I can't afford the bus fare.

When I was young, I . . .

b '**Must**' hasn't got a past tense. What verb must you use?

c Look at your chart for Exercise 3. Write down what the old man had to do and why.

Example
He had to walk to school because his parents couldn't afford the bus fare.

5 **What do you think about the old man's life? Imagine what life will be like for your grandchildren. Tell them about the hardships of your life today.**

FOLLOW UP

6 **Complete the text.**

My dad had some chickens, you .... I had to feed them .... morning and then I had .... walk to school with my .... sister. That's why I .... to get up so early. .... was two miles to school .... two miles back in the .... But it always seemed longer .... the morning, when we were .... to school. There was a ...., but we couldn't afford it.

INTERACTION

Arguments

1 **What do you argue with your parents about? Work in groups of four.**

a Write down 3 or 4 things that you argue about.

b Make a list of things that your parents say.

c Choose one of the things you argue about. Write a short play about a family argument. Your play must last only two minutes. It must have a part for every member of the group.

2 **Act out your play.**

FOLLOW UP

3 **Choose something else from Exercise 1 above and write a dialogue for another argument.**

Some interesting books

My Life of Crime
by Robin Banks

The History of Transport
by Orson Cart

Swimming the English Channel
By Francis Near

Spring is Here
by Teresa Green

Malaria
by Amos Quito

The Confessions of a Cannibal
by Henrietta Mann

The South Pole
by Anne Tarctic

The British Political System
by General E. Lection

PROJECT

Your problem page

Make a class 'problem page'.

a Work in groups. Look at the Dear Kate letters on page 92. Write a letter about another problem (real or imaginary).

b Give your letter to another group. They must write a reply.

c Display all the letters and replies as a problem page. Think up a title for each letter. Make a headline for the page.

I want to become a vegetarian because I don't believe in killing animals. How can I make sure I get a balanced diet?

How can I tell my mother kindly that I want to choose my own clothes?

I've got so much work to do that I can't concentrate at all.

I've moved to a new school and I haven't got any friends.

I've fallen in love with my best friend's girlfriend.

I came in late and my parents have grounded me.

► **Pronunciation: page 114**

Learning diary

10

1 What have you learnt in this unit? Look at the first page of the unit. How well have you achieved the learning objectives?

2 Do the self-check in the Workbook.

3 Make a problem page about learning.

Write a letter explaining a problem you have in learning English. Make a collage of letters by other people in your class.

Try to give some advice to another letter writer.

11 the truth

reported speech

Contents

Learning objectives

In this unit you will learn how to report what someone said.

Preview task

- Look through the unit. Find some examples of reported speech. How is it different from direct speech?
- Translate your examples. How does your language express reported speech?

The girl with green hair

1 What do you remember? What happened in the last part of the story? Look back at page 88 and check your ideas.

2 Look at this episode. Who are the people? Where are they? What are they doing?

3 Listen and follow in your books.

Sue Hello, Joe.

Joe Sue! What are you doing here?

Sue I've left home, Joe. We'll run away together and get married. My parents won't be able to stop us.

Joe Go home, Sue. You're just a silly schoolgirl.

Sue But, Joe. I love you. And I thought you loved me.

Joe Love you? I've never loved you and I certainly wouldn't marry you. I only went out with you because of those trees.

Girl Who's at the door, Joe? Oh ...

Joe This is Julia Kingman, my fiancee.

Later

Terry Hi, Sue. I thought I'd find you here.

Sue Hello, Terry.

Terry Have you been to Joe's place?

Sue Yes. He was very unfriendly. I said that I had left home and that we would run away together and get married. I said my parents wouldn't be able to stop us.

Terry What did he say?

Sue He told me to go home. He said I was just a silly schoolgirl. I said that I loved him. But he just laughed. He said that he had never loved me and that he certainly wouldn't marry me. And then ... then he said he had only gone out with me because of these trees.

Terry Yes, I know. Carmen saw him in town. He was with a girl at the Kingman offices. She didn't want to tell you. She thought that you would be upset. I put two and two together.

Sue Oh, Terry. I've been such a fool.

Terry Come on. Let's go home.

4 Answer these questions.

a Where has Sue gone?
b Why is Sue carrying a suitcase?
c Does Joe want to marry Sue?
d Why did Joe go out with Sue?
e Who is with Joe at his house?
f Where does Sue go after she leaves Joe's place?
g How did Terry know about Joe?
h How does Sue feel?
i Where do Sue and Terry go?

5 Close your book. Listen to the dialogue again.

Useful expressions

6 How do you say these in your language?

We'll get married. [ ]

Go home. [ ]

Who's at the door? [ ]

my fiancee [ ]

I thought I'd find you here. [ ]

He just laughed. [ ]

She didn't want to tell you. [ ]

I put two and two together. [ ]

I've been such a fool. [ ]

7 Work in groups of four. Each person takes one of the parts.

a Read the dialogue.

b Change roles and read the dialogue again.

FOLLOW UP

8 Joe is talking to Julia Kingman. Complete their conversation.

Julia That was the .... that was injured when we .... hang-gliding, wasn't it? What did .... want?

Joe She said that she .... left home and that we....... run away together and get ....

Julia Married? What.......... .... all about, Joe?

Joe Her .... is Sue and she .... in Victoria Road. I .... out with her a few times .... of those trees .... your father wants to .... down. I wanted to find out .... their protest.

Julia Oh, I see.

LANGUAGE WORK

Reported speech

1 Use the Victoria Road story to help you.

a Complete the table with the reported sentences.

direct speech Sue and Joe are talking	reported speech Sue is talking to Terry
present perfect	past perfect
'I've left home.'	I said that I had left home.
'I've never loved you.'	He said that he ....
___________	___________
'We'll run away together.'	....
___________	___________
'You're just a silly schoolgirl.'	....
'I love you.'	....
___________	___________
'I certainly wouldn't marry you.'	....
___________	___________
'I only went out with you because of those trees.'	....

b How do the tenses change? Write the names of the tenses in the spaces.

c There isn't an example of the present continuous tense in the story. What do you think it changes to in reported speech? Complete this sentence.

I'm marrying Julia.

He said that he . . .

d Find some more examples of reported speech in the story.

2 Look at the pronouns (I, you, he, etc) in the sentences above. How do they change in reported speech?

3 **This is what Carmen told Terry. Later Terry told Sue what Carmen had said. What would Terry say?**

Example
I saw Joe in town.
She said she had seen Joe in town.

a I saw Joe in town.
b He was outside the Kingman Property Company's offices.
c He went into the office.
d I followed him.
e I asked the secretary about him.
f He works for the Kingman Company.
g He is going to marry the boss's daughter.
h Her name is Julia.
i They are getting married soon.
j Joe doesn't really care for Sue.
k I don't want to tell Sue.
l Joe hasn't been to see Sue since her accident.
m She will be very upset, if I tell her.

4 **Joe said more to Sue before she left his place. This is what Sue told Kamala about it.**

He said he had only gone out with me because of the trees. I asked him what he meant. He said that he worked for the Kingman Property Company. He had only gone out with me because I lived in Victoria Road. He told me he had wanted to find out about our protest. He said that he had started the fight with Terry because the demonstration would look bad. He said that Kingman had lost. The local council had stopped them and so they weren't going to cut down the trees. So he didn't need me any more. I said that he had used me. He said that he was sorry, but he was marrying Julia and that was that.

What did Sue and Joe actually say? Start like this:

Joe 'I only went out with you because of those trees.'

Sue 'What do you mean?'

Joe 'I . . .

FOLLOW UP

5 **Write the answers to Exercise 3.**

Twelve questions about you

1 If you weren't you, who would you like to be?

2 What is your favourite activity?

3 Who would you most like to spend a holiday with? Why?

4 What makes you happy?

5 What makes you sad?

6 What do you worry about the most?

7 What is your favourite part of the day? Why?

8 Which part of the day do you like least? Why?

9 If you could have any job, what would it be?

10 If there was a competition for the 'Greatest Person in the World', who do you think should win it (apart from yourself)?

11 Apart from your parents, who has had the greatest influence on your life? How?

12 What would you most like to know about yourself?

READING

Frank's car

1 Read this. What do you think happened?

Frank Pearson was very proud of his new car, a Rover 800. It had everything — a two-litre engine, a sunroof, leather seats, electric windows. The day after he had collected the car, it was fine and sunny. So the family decided to go to Chartwood Safari Park near Birmingham. By the end of the day, Frank's car was wrecked and Frank had been arrested.

2 Now read the stories and find out what happened to Frank's car.

3 What is the missing bit of information? How did the elephant get its trunk trapped? There is a clue in the story.

4 Read the texts again. Put the pictures in the correct order to match the story.

Mr Pearson's Story

When we arrived, I parked the car and we went into the park on foot. But my mother-in-law asked whether it would be all right if she stayed in the car. She said she was feeling tired.

After we had been in the park for an hour, we heard a message over the loudspeaker. I was asked to return to my car.

When we arrived back at the car, I was horrified. The doors were damaged; one of the windows was smashed and the aerial was broken.

I asked my mother-in-law how it had happened. She said that she had been eating a sandwich, when a young elephant had poked its trunk through the open window, but she didn't remember anything after that.

I was so angry about my car. The warden gave me a glass of brandy. It was quite a large glass.

The policeman's story

At two o'clock on Wednesday 10th May we noticed Mr Pearson's car. It was damaged and we thought that it had been in an accident. We stopped Mr Pearson. I asked him whether he had been in an accident. He said that he had not. I asked him then what had happened to his car. He replied that an elephant had kicked it. At this point I noticed the smell of alcohol. I asked Mr Pearson whether he had had a drink. He said that he had had a drink of brandy. I told him that he would have to take a breathalyser test. This was positive. I then arrested Mr Pearson and took him to the police station.

The warden's story

I was sitting in my office when I heard a loud noise from the car park. I went outside. One of our elephants was trumpeting and kicking a car. I ran up to the car. The elephant's trunk was trapped in the car window. There was a lady in the car. I told her to open the window, but she had fainted. Another warden fetched a hammer. I smashed one of the windows and set the elephant free. But the elephant was so angry that it attacked the car. It kicked the wheels and pulled off the windscreen wipers and the aerial. We tried to find the owner of the car.

WORD WORK

5 Look at the picture of the car below.

a Label these parts.

windscreen wipers	window
sunroof	aerial
door	

b Use a dictionary. How many other parts can you name?

c Find words in the text for:

- the noise that an elephant makes;
- to hit with the foot;
- a test of whether a driver has drunk alcohol.

6 What do you think?

What would you do, if you were:

- Frank?
- the judge at the trial?

FOLLOW UP

7 Make a play about Frank's car.

a Work in groups. Write your play using the texts to help you.

b Act your play.

8 Tell the story of Frank's car.

LISTENING

The news

1 **Listen. You will hear a news programme.**

a Look at the pictures. What do you think the news items are about?

b Listen and check your ideas.

2 **Listen again.**

a Complete the reports.

The .... said that .... people .... injured. They also .... people .... still .... too fast in the .... weather.

A spokesman for the .... said that the .... family was .... and .... to leave the country.

A .... said that the police .... in the early hours of the morning. There .... a fight and one of .... had been injured. .... said this .... the happiest ....

The .... said last night that Gary Lineker .... fit for tomorrow's match .... England and Hungary. He .... Lineker had injured .... in a match last week. He said Lineker .... fit for the World Cup in six month's time.

b What did the people actually say?

Example
Six people have been injured.

3 How good is your memory?

a Work in pairs. Write down two things that the newscaster said about these.

- the accident
- the President
- the two bank robbers
- Linda Nairn
- Gary Lineker

Example
He said that there had been an accident on the M1. He said it had happened in thick fog.

b Compare your ideas to another pair's. Do you want to change anything?

c Listen again and check your answers.

WORD WORK

4 Look at each news item. Make a list of all the words associated with the topic of the item.

Example
news item 3

two men	*police*	*injured*
arrested	*early hours*	*fight*
bank robbery		

FOLLOW UP

5 Watch the news on TV. Write a news item in English.

INTERACTION

A news report

1 Work in groups. Choose one of the news items. If you were a newspaper editor, what other information would you like to have about the story? Decide on six questions.

Example
Where has Linda been?
Who found her?

2 Give your questions to another group. They must use the questions to make a role play.

a One member of the group is a reporter. Another member is the interviewee.

b They act the interview.

3 Each group then tells the first group what they found out.

Example
Linda said that she had gone to her grandmother's but had got lost.

FOLLOW UP

4 Use the information that your group was given in Exercise 3. Write a newspaper article about the story.

PROJECT

Here is the news

Make a news programme. It is half past eight. The news is broadcast at nine o'clock. Your news programme must be ready by nine o'clock.

a Collect news stories from TV, the radio and newspapers.

b Work in groups. One group is the news broadcasters. The other groups are reporting teams.

c Each reporting group chooses one of the stories. They write a short news item about their story. The item should include a report from a witness or spokesperson. They give their news item to the broadcasters.

d The broadcasters must prepare the news broadcast. They decide who will read the news and prepare an introduction and a conclusion. As the stories come in, they must put them in an appropriate order.

e Broadcast the news.

Learning diary

11

1 What have you learnt in this unit? Look at the first page of the unit. How well have you achieved the learning objectives?

2 Do the self-check in the Workbook.

3 You have met a lot of new vocabulary in this unit. How do you learn new words?
What helps you to learn them?
Discuss your answers with other members of your class.

► **Pronunciation: page 114**

revision 12

READING

1 Look at the picture.

a What is the animal's name? If you don't know, look quickly at the text and find its name.

b Close your book. Work in pairs. Write down everything you know about the animal.

2 Read the text and check your ideas.

a What did you know?

b What did you get wrong?

c What new information have you learnt?

d What didn't you find in the text?

Nature Profile

Sixty million years ago there were 30 species of rhinoceros on the earth. Now there are only five species and all of them are in danger of extinction. Three of the five species live in Asia. There are about 1,500 Indian one-horned rhinos in north-east India. The Sumatran rhino is the smallest of the five species. There are probably only about 800 animals left. It lives on the island of Sumatra. The rarest rhinoceros is the Javan rhino. It is found only at the western end of Java and in Kampuchea. There are only 50 Javan rhinos left.

The two African species are larger than their Asian cousins. They are the black rhino and the largest of all the rhinos, the white rhino. In fact, the white rhino is not white. It has a very wide mouth and its name comes from the Dutch word 'wijde', which means 'wide'. The white rhino eats grass, while other rhinos eat leaves. In the 1890s people thought that the white rhino was extinct. But some were found in South Africa. Since then it has been protected and there are now about 3,000. There are about 4,500 of the smaller black rhinos left.

People often think that the rhino is a slow animal, but it can run at up to 50 kilometres an hour. And it can turn very quickly. Black rhinos are very short-sighted and they can be very aggressive if people come too close to them.

Rhinoceroses are large animals. The black rhino weighs between 1 and 1.5 tonnes and an adult white rhino can weigh 3 tonnes. They have very thick skins, too. As a result, they have no natural enemies. Their only enemy is Man. But Man is the worst enemy of all.

Rhinos are hunted for their horns. It is not a real horn. It is made of hair. It is used in traditional Chinese medicines for colds, headaches and many other illnesses. In the Yemen, men carry a traditional knife called a 'jambiyya'. The handles of the most expensive 'jambiyya' are made of rhino horn. In the 1970s a lot of Yemeni men became richer because they went to work in countries like Saudi Arabia. As a result, many more men could afford knives with rhino horn handles. Ninety per cent of the black rhinos in East Africa were killed by poachers in the 1970s.

Rhinos are protected in most African countries, but many animals are still killed by poachers. By the year 2,000 the Javan rhino will be seen only in museums and books. Will its African cousins share the same fate?

3 **Here are the five species of rhino.**

a Which is which?

b Name the places on the map where the rhinos live.

c Write two facts about each species of rhino.

4 **Complete the graph.**

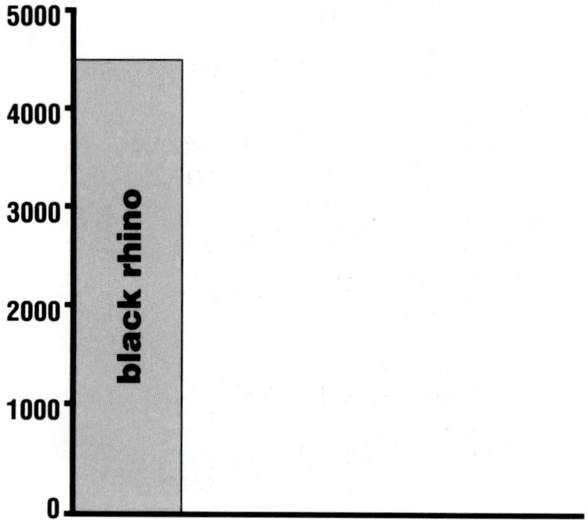

5 **Read the text again and find the answers to the questions.**

a Why are rhinos hunted?
b What is the horn made of?
c What is the horn used for?
d Why did hunting rise in the 1970s?
e Why do you think the Asian rhinos are the rarest?

6 **What do you think?**

If the rhinos became extinct, would you care? Would you give any money to save the rhinos?

FOLLOW UP

7 **Write down everything you have learnt from the text about the black rhino.**

LISTENING

The future

1 **What does the future hold for Sue and Terry? What do you think will happen?**

Work in groups. Write a final episode called: 'The future'.

Your play must:

- have a part for every member of your group;
- be no more than two minutes long;
- contain at least five expressions from the Useful expressions sections.

2 **Act out your play.**

3 **Listen to the final episode. Compare it to your play. Is it the same?**

FOLLOW UP

4 **What does the future hold for you? What are you going to do with your life? Write about what you are going to do.**

Listen to the song 'The Leaving of Liverpool'.

WRITING

Sue is writing to Carmen. She tells Carmen about everything that has happened since Carmen went home. Write Sue's letter. Try to report what people said as much as possible.

Learning diary

12

You've come to the end of this book. But it's not the end of learning English.

How do you feel about the things that you have learnt?

Look back at the Learning diaries in the book. Write down three things:

- that you think you know well now.
- that you are still not sure about.
- that you really enjoyed.
- that you think you will remember most.

Discuss your lists with other members of your class.

Good luck with your next year of English!

▶ Pronunciation: page 114

SURVIVAL
Can the world survive?
5
6
7
Several species of fish and marine mammals are threatened by over-fishing. Go back to the start.
8
9
10
11
An international fund is set up to save the Amazon rain forest. Double your next throw.
12
13
14
15
A tropical rain forest is flooded and destroyed when a new dam is built. Go back five spaces.
16
17
18
An oil tanker sinks. Two hundred kilometres of coastline are polluted. Go back to 8.
19
20
21
22
23
Two baby pandas are born in zoos. Go forward two spaces.
24
25
26
A ship carrying poisonous waste sinks. All marine life along the European coast is threatened. Stay here till you throw an even number.
27
28
29
Drought. Millions of animals and people face starvation. Go back four spaces.
30
33
34
35
A gang of ivory poachers is caught. Have another throw.
72
73
The import of tropical hardwood is banned by the EEC. Go to 75.
74
75
76
Dumping waste in the North Sea causes diseases in fish and shellfish. Go back to 68.

FINISH
77
78
79
Two countries start hunting whales again. Go back to 63.
58
57
All drift net fishing is banned worldwide. Go forward three spaces.
71
The breeding grounds of turtles and seals are disturbed by tourists. Three species face extinction. Go back to 61.
The destruction of the Himalayan forest causes huge floods in the Ganges delta. Thousands of animals and people die. Go back five spaces.
59
0
56
53
55
69
68
67
54
60
Millions of sea birds are killed by an oil slick. Miss a turn.
52
The world's population reaches six billion. Go back to 48.
A thousand square kilometres of rain forest is destroyed to make chopsticks. Go back to 37.
31
61
51
66
62
50
65
63
Indian tigers are protected in a new national park. Double your next throw.
46
32
64
49
47
45
A species of plant that could cure AIDS becomes extinct. Go back ten spaces.
The last Sumatran rhino is killed. Miss a turn.
48
44
39
40
43
36
37
38
All whaling is banned. Go forward two spaces.
42
41
Two rare species of birds are threatened by egg collectors. Miss a turn.
Antarctica is declared a World Park. Go forward three spaces.
1
START
3
4
2

PRONUNCIATION PRACTICE

Introduction Phonetic alphabet revision: vowels

These are the vowel sounds of English.

a **Listen and repeat.**

/i:/	seen	....	/ju:/	new	....
/ɪ/	disk	....	/ɜ:/	word	....
/e/	get	....	/ə/	over	....
/æ/	can	....	/eɪ/	stay	....
/ɑ:/	dark	....	/aɪ/	five	....
/ʌ/	fun	....	/ɔɪ/	toy	....
/ɒ/	dog	....	/aʊ/	now	....
/ɔ:/	saw	....	/əʊ/	road	....
/ʊ/	foot	....	/eə/	care	....
/u:/	moon	....	/ɪə/	dear	....

b **Write these words next to the correct sound in the second column.**

write	red	tin	May	near
music	leave	don't	do	look
cut	sport	black	class	hair
town	third	job	noise	the

Unit 1 /ɑ:/, /æ/

a **Look at these words.**

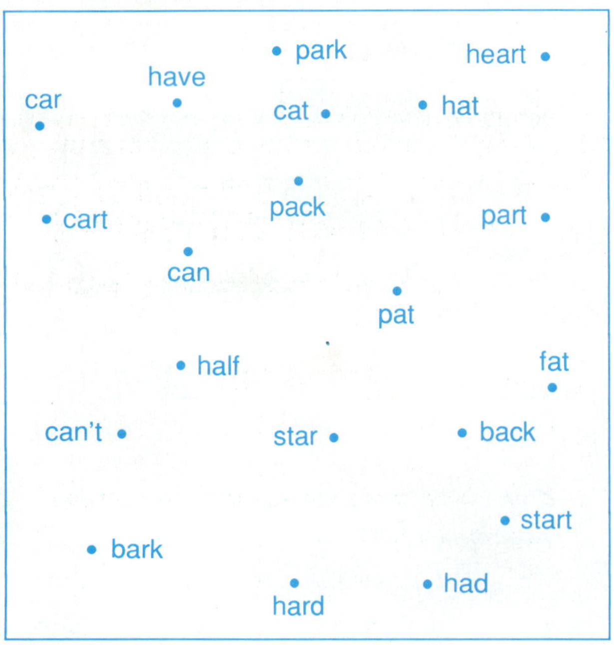

b **Listen. Draw a line to connect the words that you hear. What shape do you get?**

c **Listen again and repeat the words.**

d **How do you say the other words?**

e **Put the words in the right column.**

/ɑ:/	/æ/

Unit 2 /ɒ/, /ɔ:/

What shape can you find?

a **Look at the diagram below. Each number represents a word on the tape. Some of the words have an /ɒ/ sound and some have an /ɔ:/ sound.**

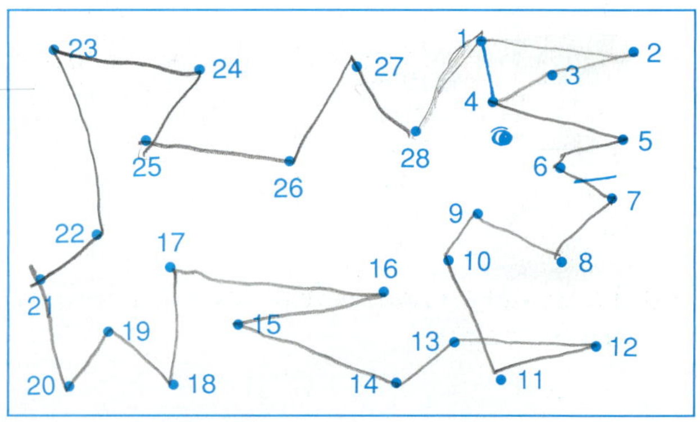

b **Listen. You will hear the words. Put your pencil on the dot of the first word with an /ɒ/ sound. When you hear another word with an /ɒ/ sound, draw a line to that dot. If you hear an /ɔ:/ sound, don't draw a line. When you have connected all the /ɒ/ words, you will find the shape.**

Example
1 job /dʒɒb/: put your pencil on dot 1
2 bored /bɔ:d/: wait for the next word
3 saw /sɔ:/: wait for the next word
4 was /wɒz/: draw a line from 1 to 4

c **Listen again and repeat.**

Unit 3 Rhymes

a **Match the rhymes. Use a dictionary to help you. In each line there are two sets, one with two words that rhyme and one with three words that rhyme.**

bass	face	vase	case	stars
there	fair	here	bear	near
lead	lead	need	dead	red

b **Listen and check your ideas.**

c **What do you notice about 'lead'? Do you know another word like this?**

Unit 4 Phonetic alphabet revision: consonants

a **Most consonants have the same symbol in the phonetic alphabet as in the ordinary alphabet.**

Example
book /bʊk/

But these symbols are special. Match them to the correct word.

/ð/	join
/ʃ/	long
/ʒ/	three
/tʃ/	push
/dʒ/	these
/θ/	treasure
/ŋ/	chair

b **These are all names from this unit. What are the names?**

/'dʒeɪsən/ ....

/'kɜːlɪ/ ....

/ˌmaɪkl 'greɪd/ ....

/ʃɑː'liːn/ ....

/ˌlɪtl 'iːvə/ ....

/ðə ˌləʊkə'məʊʃn/ ....

/ˌmædʒ 'mɪtʃl/ ....

/ˌkɒrə'neɪʃn striːt/ ....

/'kaɪlɪ/ ....

/'ælɪsən/ ....

Unit 5 /d/, /t/

Is the final sound /d/ or /t/?
Listen. If the final sound is /d/, repeat the word. If it is /t/, stay silent.

Unit 6 /s/

Listen and repeat.

Spain	stereo	skiing
sprain	cycle	summer
spoonful	sling	sore throat
stomach	seat belt	skin
safe		

Say this:

> She sells sea shells on the sea shore. The sea shells that she sells are sea shells, I'm sure.

Unit 7 /s/, /z/

a **Before you listen, put these words in the correct column.**

bra**c**elet	watche**s**	offi**c**e
re**s**in	water re**s**istant	recogni**z**e
second	sale**s**man	**s**ell
style	pri**c**e	Chine**s**e
ca**s**e		

/s/	/z/

b **Listen. Can you hear a /s/ sound or a /z/ sound? Do you want to move any of the words?**

c **Listen again and check your answers.**

Unit 8 Phonetic alphabet revision

a **Complete these words with the correct phonetic symbols.**

/h.........d/	heard	/w......../	wash
/iː.........ɪ/	easy	/......uː..../	juice
/w......kɪ..../	walking	/w......d....../	wouldn't
/....r..../	through	/........ɪk/	quick
/d......../	down	/mɑː........./	March

b Write these words in phonetic symbols.

Joe	....	his	....
was	....	knife	....
ninth	....	food	....
worst	....	wood	....
anything	....	cough	....

Unit 9 /ʃ/, /tʃ/, /dʒ/

a Listen and repeat.

Washington	watch	kitchen
Manchester	crash	ostrich
Los Angeles	digital	change
Chicago	shock	travel agency
spaceship	wish	check-in
baggage	Joe	station

b Put the words into the correct check-in desk.

c Listen again and check your ideas.

Unit 10 /u:/, /ʊ/

What shape can you find?

a Look at the diagram. Each number represents a word on the tape. Some of the words have an /u:/ sound and some have an /ʊ/ sound.

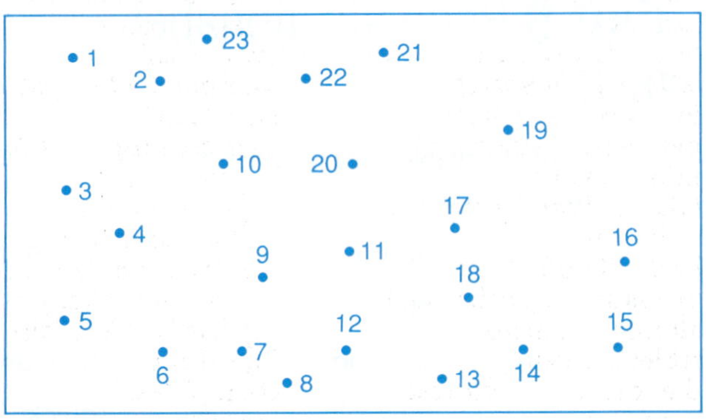

b Listen. You will hear the words. Put your pencil on the dot of the first word with an /u:/ sound. When you hear another word with an /u:/ sound, draw a line to that dot. If you hear an /ʊ/ sound, don't draw a line. When you have connected the /u:/ words, you will find the shape.

c Say these.

school rules	a good food book
blue wool	The school is full of fools
Put your foot in the boot	

Unit 11 Consonant clusters

a Listen and repeat.

trapped	damaged	loudspeaker
smashed	laughed	electric
fetched	sandwich	through
asked	breathalyser	trunk
stopped	protest	

b Say these.

He laughed and laughed and laughed.
It kicked, smashed and damaged the car.
I asked what had happened.

Unit 12 A secret message

Here is a message for Terry. What does it say? Write it in words.

/ju: ʃʊd ˌdʒɔɪn ðə ˌʃɪp ət ˌpɔ:tsməθ ˈhɑ:bər

....

æt ˌkwɔ:tə pɑ:st ˈθri: ɒn ˌwenzdɪ ðə ˌθɜ:d əv ˈdʒu:n

....

pli:z ˌdəʊnt brɪŋ ˌtu: mʌtʃ ˈbægɪdʒ

....

ˌɪf jə ˌhæv enɪ ˈkwestʃənz

....

pli:z ˌfəʊn aʊr ˌɒfɪs ɪn ˈlʌndən/

....

WORDLIST

INTRODUCTION

enjoy /ɪn'dʒɔɪ/
newspaper /'nju:speɪpə(r)/
these days /'ði:z deɪz/
Physics /'fɪzɪks/
Chemistry /'kemɪstrɪ/
Computer Studies /kəm'pju:tə stʌdɪz/
often /'ɒfn/
lately /'leɪtlɪ/
since /sɪns/
college /'kɒlɪdʒ/
recognize /'rekəgnaɪz/
at first /ət 'fɜ:st/
Guess what. /ges 'wɒt/
still /stɪl/
learn /lɜ:n/
I've got to . . . /aɪv ˌgɒt tə ' . . ./
impossible /ɪm'pɒsəbl/
stand back /stænd 'bæk/

---

leave school /li:v 'sku:l/
fed up with . . . /fed 'ʌp wɪð . . ./
earn /ɜ:n/
study /'stʌdɪ/
go out with . . . /gəʊ ˌaʊt wɪð ' . . ./
I suppose . . . /aɪ sə'pəʊz/
school leaving party /sku:l 'li:vɪŋ pɑ:tɪ/

---

gossip /'gɒsɪp/
scandal /'skændl/

UNIT 1 LIFESTYLES

park /pɑ:k/
make it /'meɪk ɪt/
key /ki:/
smart /smɑ:t/
sports car /'spɔ:ts kɑ:(r)/
rush /rʌʃ/
hide /haɪd/
tell /tel/
bore /bɔ:(r)/
office /'ɒfɪs/
belong to . . . /bɪ'lɒŋ tə . . ./
group /gru:p/
any more /ənɪ 'mɔ:(r)/
I know what you mean. /aɪ ˌnəʊ wɒt ju: 'mi:n/
look out /lʊk 'aʊt/
mention /'menʃn/
remind /rɪ'maɪnd/

---

exciting /ɪk'saɪtɪŋ/
boring /'bɔ:rɪŋ/

---

imagine /ɪ'mædʒɪn/
without /wɪð'aʊt/
electricity /ɪˌlek'trɪsətɪ/
industry /'ɪndəstrɪ/
on foot /ɒn 'fʊt/
century /'sentʃərɪ/
perhaps /pə'hæps/
lifestyle /'laɪfstaɪl/
among /ə'mʌŋ/
ancestor /'ænsestə(r)/
base /beɪs/
Bible /'baɪbl/
tractor /'træktə(r)/
village /'vɪlɪdʒ/
strict /strɪkt/
plain /pleɪn/
bonnet /'bɒnɪt/
jewellery /'dʒu:əlrɪ/
set /set/
such as . . . /ˌsʌtʃ æz ' . . ./
barn /bɑ:n/
lift /lɪft/
hammer /'hæmə(r)/
prepare /prɪ'peə(r)/
musical instrument /ˌmju:zɪkl 'ɪnstrʊmənt/
hymn /hɪm/
chemical /'kemɪkl/
rule /ru:l/
crime /kraɪm/
pollution /pə'lu:ʃn/

---

speaking /'spi:kɪŋ/
I can't make it. /aɪ ˌkɑ:nt 'meɪk ɪt/
What about . . . ? /wɒt əˌbaʊt ' . . ./
How about . . . ? /haʊ əˌbaʊt ' . . ./
afterwards /'ɑ:ftəwədz/
free /fri:/
important /ɪm'pɔ:tənt/
problem /'prɒbləm/
influence /'ɪnflʊəns/
kind /kaɪnd/
I don't care. /'aɪ dəʊnt keə(r)/
meant /ment/

---

argument /'ɑ:gjʊmənt/
make arrangements /ˌmeɪk ə'reɪndʒmənts/
explain /ɪk'spleɪn/
arrange /ə'reɪndʒ/
feelings /'fi:lɪŋz/

---

cart /kɑ:t/
part /pɑ:t/

UNIT 2 TURNING POINTS

super /'su:pə(r)/
secret /'si:krɪt/
promise /'prɒmɪs/
wonderful /'wʌndəfl/
Steady on. /ˌstedɪ 'ɒn/
excited /ɪk'saɪtɪd/
guy /gaɪ/
before /bɪ'fɔ:(r)/
mostly /'məʊstlɪ/
ask . . . out /ˌɑ:sk . . . 'aʊt/
get off . . . /ˌget ɒf ' . . ./
by /baɪ/
the pictures /ðə 'pɪktʃəz/
ancient /'eɪnʃənt/
have a look /ˌhæv ə 'lʊk/
reach /ri:tʃ/
turning point /'tɜ:nɪŋ pɔɪnt/

---

whenever /wen'evə(r)/
pink /pɪŋk/
elephants /'elɪfənts/
have coffee with . . . /hæv 'kɒfɪ wɪð . . ./
fall in love /ˌfɔ:l ɪn 'lʌv/
have an argument /ˌhæv ən 'ɑ:gjʊmənt/
do your community work /ˌdu: jɔ: kə'mju:nətɪ wɜ:k/

---

claim /kleɪm/
throne /θrəʊn/
earl /ɜ:l/
duke /dju:k/
Norway /'nɔ:weɪ/
Normandy /'nɔ:məndɪ/
attack /ə'tæk/
on the top of . . . /ɒn ðə 'tɒp əv . . ./
pretend /prɪ'tend/
knight /naɪt/
kill /kɪl/
end /end/
army /ɑ:mɪ/
destroy /dɪ'strɔɪ/
rest /rest/
battle /'bætl/
coast /kəʊst/
march /mɑ:tʃ/
crown /kraʊn/
conqueror /'kɒŋkərə(r)/
language /'læŋgwɪdʒ/
cousin /'kʌzn/
grow up /grəʊ 'ʌp/
soldier /'səʊldʒə(r)/
ruler /'ru:lə(r)/
archer /'ɑ:tʃə(r)/
fire /'faɪə(r)/
arrow /'ærəʊ/
look up /lʊk 'ʌp/
win /wɪn/
won /wʌn/
giant /'dʒaɪənt/
reply /rɪ'plaɪ/
grave /greɪv/
challenge /'tʃælɪndʒ/

---

kind of . . . /kaɪnd əv ' . . ./
take a chance /ˌteɪk ə 'tʃɑ:ns/
hold . . . tight /ˌhəʊld . . . 'taɪt/
star /stɑ:(r)/
shine /ʃaɪn/
bright /braɪt/
kiss /kɪs/
let . . . know /ˌlet . . . 'nəʊ/
whisper /'wɪspə(r)/
in a way /ˌɪn ə 'weɪ/
evermore /ˌevə'mɔ:(r)/
mine /maɪn/
take . . . home /ˌteɪk . . . 'həʊm/
bride /braɪd/
by his side /ˌbaɪ hɪz 'saɪd/
almost /'ɔ:lməʊst/
tablet /'tæblɪt/
the rest of . . . /ðə 'rest əv . . ./
effect /ɪ'fekt/

UNIT 3 PEOPLE

lovely /'lʌvlɪ/
sound like /'saʊnd laɪk/
the truth /ðə 'tru:θ/
the sooner the better /ðə ˌsu:nə ðə 'betə(r)/
sooner or later /ˌsu:nər ɔ: 'leɪtə(r)/
be late for . . . /bɪ 'leɪt fə(r) . . ./
nobody else /ˌnəʊbədɪ 'els/
stand a chance /ˌstænd ə 'tʃɑ:ns/
Go on with you. /gəʊ 'ɒn wɪð ˌju:/
the other evening /ðɪ ˌʌðər 'i:vnɪŋ/

---

personality test /ˌpɜ:sə'nælətɪ test/
the centre of attention /ðə ˌsentər ɒv ə'tenʃn/
prefer /prɪ'fɜ:(r)/
on your own /ˌɒn jɔ:r 'əʊn/
profile /'prəʊfaɪl/
cameraman /'kæmrəmæn/
camerawoman /'kæmrəwʊmən/
writer /'raɪtə(r)/
director /dɪ'rektə(r)/
member /'membə(r)/
bass guitar /ˌbeɪs gɪ'tɑ:(r)/
lead guitar /ˌli:d gɪ'tɑ:(r)/
drums /drʌmz/
mind /maɪnd/
scientist /'saɪəntɪst/
politician /ˌpɒlɪ'tɪʃn/
score /skɔ:(r)/
practical /'præktɪkl/
engineer /ˌendʒɪ'nɪə(r)/
a loner /ə 'ləʊnə(r)/
interested in . . . /'ɪntrɪstɪd ɪn . . ./
stage /steɪdʒ/
artist /'ɑ:tɪst/
natural /'nætʃrəl/
direct /dɪ'rekt/
business executive /'bɪznɪs ɪgzekjʊtɪv/
image /'ɪmɪdʒ/
model /'mɒdl/
dominant /'dɒmɪnənt/
balanced /'bælənst/

---

dress sense /'dres sens/
what is . . . like? /ˌwɒt ɪz ' . . . laɪk/
style /staɪl/
look good /'lʊk gʊd/
suit /su:t/
This goes for . . . /ˌðɪs gəʊz fə(r) ' . . ./
experiment (*v.*) /ɪk'sperɪment/
Don't be afraid of . . . /ˌdəʊnt bɪ ə'freɪd əv . . ./
especially /ɪ'speʃəlɪ/
hips /hɪps/
chest /tʃest/
bust /bʌst/
pattern /'pætn/

slim /slɪm/
stripe /straɪp/
vertical /'vɜ:tɪkl/
lamp post /'læmp pəʊst/
horizontal /ˌhɒrɪ'zɒntl/
opposite /'ɒpəsɪt/
effect /ɪ'fekt/
shoulder /'ʃəʊldə(r)/
broad /brɔ:d/
narrow /'nærəʊ/
waist /weɪst/
loose /lu:s/
bottom /'bɒtəm/
baggy /'bægɪ/
draw attention to . . . /drɔ: ə'tenʃn tə . . ./
ideal /aɪ'di:l/
hint /hɪnt/
outfit /'aʊtfɪt/
look your best /ˌlʊk jɔ: 'best/

---

hero /'hɪərəʊ/
heroine /'herəʊɪn/
admire /əd'maɪə(r)/
dislike /dɪs'laɪk/
collage /'kɒlɑ:ʒ/
be like . . . /ˌbɪ: laɪk '. . ./

---

vase /vɑ:z/
planet /'plænɪt/
zoo /zu:/
lead (*n., adj.*) /led/
heavier /'hevɪə(r)/
iron /'aɪən/

UNIT 4 REVISION

soap opera /'səʊp ɒprə/
lunchtime /'lʌntʃtaɪm/
popular /'pɒpjʊlə(r)/
favourite /'feɪvrɪt/
controller /kən'trəʊlə(r)/
secretly /'si:krɪtlɪ/
audience /'ɔ:dɪəns/
population /ˌpɒpjʊ'leɪʃn/
play the part of . . . /ˌpleɪ ðə ˌpɑ:t əv '. . ./
big break /bɪg 'breɪk/
career /kə'rɪə(r)/
remake (*n.*) /'ri:meɪk/
the charts /ðə 'tʃɑ:ts/
strong-willed /ˌstrɒŋ'wɪld/
impatient /ɪm'peɪʃənt/
appear /ə'pɪə(r)/
celebrate /'selɪbreɪt/
wedding /'wedɪŋ/
delinquent /dɪ'lɪŋkwənt/
certain /'sɜ:tn/
down under /ˌdaʊn 'ʌndə(r)/

---

repeat /rɪ'pi:t/
character /'kærəktə(r)/
nickname /'nɪkneɪm/
straight /streɪt/
joke /dʒəʊk/
good-looking /ˌgʊd'lʊkɪŋ/
married /'mærɪd/
clever /'klevə(r)/
serious /'sɪərɪəs/
properly /'prɒpəlɪ/
romantic /rəʊ'mæntɪk/

curly /'kɜ:lɪ/

---

invent /ɪn'vent/
relationship /rɪ'leɪʃnʃɪp/
background /'bækgraʊnd/

UNIT 5 PROTEST

demo /'deməʊ/
leaflet /'li:flɪt/
permission /pə'mɪʃn/
property /'prɒpətɪ/
land /lænd/
plant /plɑ:nt/
Napoleon /nə'pəʊlɪən/
unless /ən'les/
local /'ləʊkl/
council /'kaʊnsl/
petition /pə'tɪʃn/
demonstration /'demən'streɪʃn/
support /sə'pɔ:t/
placard /'plækɑ:d/
banner /'bænə(r)/
sign /saɪn/
the more the merrier /ðə ˌmɔ: ðə 'merɪə(r)/
pole /pəʊl/
let go of . . . /let ˌgəʊ əv '. . ./
police station /pə'li:s steɪʃn/
poster /'pəʊstə(r)/

Suffragette /ˌsʌfrə'dʒet/
vote /vəʊt/
march /mɑ:tʃ/
peaceful /'pi:sfl/
violent /'vaɪələnt/
interrupt /ˌɪntə'rʌpt/
sentence /'sentəns/
release /rɪ'li:s/
hunger strike /'hʌŋgə straɪk/
chain /tʃeɪn/
railings /'reɪlɪŋz/

---

rain forest /'reɪn fɒrɪst/
hectare /'hekteə(r)/
reason /'ri:zn/
crop /krɒp/
firewood /'faɪəwʊd/
export (*v.*) /ek'spɔ:t/
Japan /dʒə'pæn/
furniture /'fɜ:nɪtʃə(r)/
unfortunately /ʌn'fɔ:tʃənətlɪ/
replace /rɪ'pleɪs/
soil /sɔɪl/
protect /prə'tekt/
wash away . . . /ˌwɒʃ əweɪ '. . ./
rain /reɪn/
blow away . . . /'bləʊ əweɪ '. . ./
wind (*n.*) /wɪnd/
grow /grəʊ/
desert /'dezət/
destroy /dɪ'strɔɪ/
lose /lu:z/
plant /plɑ:nt/
species /'spi:ʃɪz/
extinct /ɪk'stɪŋkt/
reptile /'reptaɪl/
mammal /'mæml/

insect /'ɪnsekt/
shellfish /'ʃelfɪʃ/
as well as . . . /əz ˌwel əz '. . ./
Who is to blame? /ˌhu: ɪz tə 'bleɪm/
disaster /dɪ'zɑ:stə(r)/
billion /'bɪlɪən/
hi-fi /'haɪfaɪ/
teak /ti:k/
loudspeaker /ˌlaʊd'spi:kə(r)/
mahogany /mə'hɒgənɪ/
destruction /dɪ'strʌkʃn/
marsh /mɑ:ʃ/
environment /ɪn'vaɪərənmənt/

---

tropical /'trɒpɪkl/
recently /'ri:səntlɪ/
peaceful /'pi:sfl/
leader /'lɪ:də(r)/
describe /dɪ'skraɪb/
hunt /hʌnt/
wild animal /ˌwaɪld 'ænɪml/
jungle /'dʒʌŋgl/
shatter /'ʃætə(r)/
timber /'tɪmbə(r)/
one third /ˌwʌn 'θɜ:d/
pollute /pə'lu:t/
mud /mʌd/
frighten away /ˌfraɪtn ə'weɪ/
saw /sɔ:/
lorry /'lɒrɪ/
blockade /blɒ'keɪd/
block /blɒk/
so far . . . /'səʊ fɑ:(r) . . ./
expect /ɪk'spekt/
trust /trʌst/
provide /prə'vaɪd/
a matter of life and death /ə ˌmætər əv ˌlaɪf ən 'deθ/
choice /tʃɔɪs/

---

corrupt /kə'rʌpt/
greedy /'gri:dɪ/
advice /əd'vaɪs/

---

protest (*adj., n.*) /'prəʊtest/
protest (*v.*) /prə'test/
issue /'ɪʃu:/

---

campaign /kæm'peɪn/

UNIT 6 DANGER

hang-gliding /'hæŋglaɪdɪŋ/
dangerous /'deɪndʒərəs/
hobby /'hɒbɪ/
snake charming /'sneɪk tʃɑ:mɪŋ/
crocodile wrestling /'krɒkədaɪl reslɪŋ/
jealous /'dʒeləs/
pass an exam /ˌpɑ:s ən ɪg'zæm/
plenty of . . . /'plentɪ əv . . ./

give . . . a lift /gɪv ˌ. . . ə 'lɪft/
look like . . . /ˌlʊk laɪk '. . ./
have a go /ˌhæv ə 'gəʊ/
get down /get 'daʊn/
crash /kræʃ/
announce /ə'naʊns/
arrival /ə'raɪvl/
flight /flaɪt/

---

skiing /'ski:ɪŋ/
sunbathing /'sʌnbeɪðɪŋ/
jogging /'dʒɒgɪŋ/
doing housework /ˌdu:ɪŋ 'haʊswɜ:k/
taking photographs /ˌteɪkɪŋ 'fəʊtəgrɑ:fs/

---

taxi /'tæksɪ/
lift /lɪft/
information desk /ˌɪnfə'meɪʃn desk/

---

horse racing /'hɔ:s reɪsɪŋ/
motor racing /'məʊtə reɪsɪŋ/
nuclear /'nju:klɪə(r)/
power station /'paʊə steɪʃn/
probably /'prɒbəblɪ/
motorbike /'məʊtəbaɪk/
risk /rɪsk/
accident /'æksɪdənt/
object (*v.*) /ɒb'dʒekt/
accept /æk'sept/
publicity /pʌb'lɪsətɪ/
run a risk /ˌrʌn ə 'rɪsk/
motorcyclist /'məʊtəsaɪklɪst/
horrific /hə'rɪfɪk/
in spite of . . . /ɪn ˌspaɪt əv '. . ./
fear /fɪə(r)/
common /'kɒmən/
benefit /'benɪfɪt/
safe /seɪf/
death /deθ/
heart disease /'hɑ:t dɪzi:z/
lung cancer /'lʌŋ kænsə(r)/
for example /fər ɪg'zɑ:mpl/
crash helmet /'kræʃ helmɪt/
seat belt /'si:t belt/
age /eɪdʒ/
involve /ɪn'vɒlv/
skin cancer /'skɪn kænsə(r)/
healthy /'helθɪ/
beautiful /'bju:tɪfl/
unnecessary /ʌn'nesəsərɪ/

---

a broken arm /ə ˌbrəʊkən 'ɑ:m/
a sore throat /ə ˌsɔ: 'θrəʊt/
earache /'ɪəreɪk/
a sprained ankle /ə ˌspreɪnd 'æŋkl/
a rash /ə ræʃ/
toothache /'tu:θeɪk/
flu /flu:/
a cough /ə 'kɒf/

a cold /ə 'kəʊld/
a temperature /ə 'temprɪtʃə(r)/
a headache /ə 'hedeɪk/
feel well /'fi:l wel/
mouth /maʊθ/
tongue /tʌŋ/
prescription /prɪ'skrɪpʃn/
spoonful /'spu:nfʊl/
every four hours /ˌevrɪ ˌfɔ:r 'aʊəz/
keep warm /ki:p 'wɔ:m/
take off . . . /ˌteɪk ɒf '. . ./
fall over /fɔ:l 'əʊvə(r)/
sprain /spreɪn/
x-ray /'eksreɪ/
bandage /'bændɪdʒ/
plaster /'plɑ:stə(r)/
sling /slɪŋ/
injection /ɪndʒekʃn/
drops /drɒps/
medicine /'medsɪn/

sea shell /'si: ʃel/
sea shore /'si: ʃɔ:(r)/

UNIT 7 COPING

How do I get to . . . ? /ˌhaʊ du: aɪ ˌget tə '. . ./
on your own /ˌɒn jɔ:r 'əʊn/
There was no reply. /ˌðeə wəz ˌnəʊ rɪ'plaɪ/
by train /baɪ 'treɪn/
suitcase /'su:tkeɪs/
There's nobody in. /ðeəz ˌnəʊbɒdɪ 'ɪn/
What's up? /wɒts 'ʌp/
my place /'maɪ pleɪs/
correct (*v.*) /kə'rekt/
ambulance /'æmbjʊləns/

annoy /ə'nɔɪ/
litter /'lɪtə(r)/
out of order /ˌaʊt əv 'ɔ:də(r)/

digital /'dɪdʒɪtl/
calculator /'kælkjʊleɪtə(r)/
resin /'rezɪn/
case /keɪs/
strap /stræp/
display /dɪ'spleɪ/
alarm /ə'lɑ:m/
function /'fʌŋkʃn/
feature /'fi:tʃə(r)/
guaranteed /ˌgærən'ti:d/
special offer /ˌspeʃl 'ɒfə(r)/
recommended /ˌrekə'mendɪd/
price /praɪs/
dual /'dju:əl/
analogue /'ænəlɒg/
dial /'daɪəl/
setting /'setɪŋ/
movement /'mu:vmənt/
stainless steel /ˌsteɪnlɪs 'sti:l/
bracelet /'breɪslɪt/
water resistant /'wɔ:tə rɪzɪstənt/
gold plated /gəʊld 'pleɪtɪd/
chrome plated /krəʊm 'pleɪtɪd/
hourly /'aʊəlɪ/
chime /tʃaɪm/
round /raʊnd/
square /skweə(r)/
face /feɪs/
diver /'daɪvə(r)/
gold trim /gəʊld 'trɪm/
luminous /'lu:mɪnəs/
markings /'mɑ:kɪŋz/
rubber /'rʌbə(r)/
protection /prə'tekʃn/
shock resistant /'ʃɒk rɪzɪstənt/
stopwatch /'stɒpwɒtʃ/
countdown /'kaʊntdaʊn/
lap /læp/
accurate /'ækjʊrət/
roman /'rəʊmən/
numerals /'nju:mərəlz/
leather /'leðə(r)/
elasticated /ɪ'læstɪkeɪtɪd/
fabric /'fæbrɪk/
pop swatch /'pɒp swɒtʃ/
catalogue /'kætəlɒg/

parcel /'pɑ:sl/
string /strɪŋ/
tie /taɪ/
flat /flæt/
Sellotape /'seləteɪp/
roll /rəʊl/
round /raʊnd/
draw /drɔ:/
shop assistant /'ʃɒp əsɪstənt/
factory /'fæktrɪ/
salesman /'seɪlzmən/
magpie /'mægpaɪ/
penguin /'pengwɪn/
Antarctic /æn'tɑ:ktɪk/
ostrich /'ɒstrɪtʃ/
saucepan /'sɔ:spən/
cook /kʊk/
recipe /'resəpɪ/
scales /skeɪlz/
socket /'sɒkɪt/
plug /plʌg/
cushion /'kʊʃn/
pillow /'pɪləʊ/
shoelaces /'ʃu:leɪsɪz/
buckle /'bʌkl/
zip /zɪp/
button /'bʌtn/
peacock /'pi:kɒk/
drawing pin /'drɔ:ɪŋ pɪn/
glue /glu:/
frying pan /'fraɪɪŋ pæn/
bank clerk /'bæŋk klɑ:k/

electrical /ɪ'lektrɪkl/
sticky /'stɪkɪ/
human /'hju:mən/
plastic /'plæstɪk/
pointed /'pɔɪntɪd/
metal /'metl/

UNIT 8 REVISION

advertising /'ædvətaɪzɪŋ/
drugs /drʌgz/
sponsor /'spɒnsə(r)/
advertise /'ædvətaɪz/
athlete /'æθli:t/
disqualify /dɪ'skwɒlɪfaɪ/
medal /'medl/
sponsorship /'spɒnsəʃɪp/
golf course /'gɒlf kɔ:s/
pitch /pɪtʃ/
equipment /ɪ'kwɪpmənt/
boxing ring /'bɒksɪŋ rɪŋ/
prize /praɪz/
glamorous /'glæmərəs/
snooker /'snu:kə(r)/
club /klʌb/
fee /fi:/
publicity /pʌb'lɪsətɪ/
image /'ɪmɪdʒ/
track /træk/
racing circuit /'reɪsɪŋ sɜ:kɪt/
champion /'tʃæmpɪən/
skier /'ski:ə(r)/

according to . . . /əˌkɔ:dɪŋ tə '. . ./
survey (*n.*) /'sɜ:veɪ/
You're kidding! /jʊə 'kɪdɪŋ/
activity /æk'tɪvətɪ/
go round to . . . /gəʊ ˌraʊnd tə '. . ./
judo /'dʒu:dəʊ/
hoover /'hu:və(r)/
window shopping /'wɪndəʊ ʃɒpɪŋ/
babysit /'beɪbɪsɪt/
typical /'tɪpɪkl/
part-time job /ˌpɑ:t taɪm 'dʒɒb/

birthday (*n.*) /'bɜ:θdeɪ/
indestructible /ˌɪndɪ'strʌktɪbl/
dustproof /'dʌstpru:f/

go on a diet /ˌgəʊ ɒn ə 'daɪət/
fitter /'fɪtə(r)/
cheating /'tʃi:tɪŋ/
bankrupt /'bæŋkrʌpt/

UNIT 9 UP, UP AND AWAY

discovery /dɪ'skʌvərɪ/
travel agency /'trævl eɪdʒənsɪ/
return flight /rɪˌtɜ:n 'flaɪt/
cost /kɒst/
special /'speʃl/
fare /feə(r)/
after all /ˌɑ:ftər 'ɔ:l/
a pity /ə 'pɪtɪ/
disappointed /ˌdɪsə'pɔɪntɪd/

Japanese /ˌdʒæpə'ni:z/

competition /ˌkɒmpə'tɪʃn/
winner /'wɪnə(r)/
fly-drive /'flaɪdraɪv/
statue /'stætʃu:/
holiday of a lifetime /ˌhɒlɪdeɪ ˌɒv ə 'laɪftaɪm/
pick up . . . /ˌpɪk ʌp '. . ./
the Deep South /ðə ˌdi:p 'saʊθ/
believe /bɪ'li:v/
answer /'ɑ:nsə(r)/
fill in . . . /ˌfɪl ɪn '. . ./
post /pəʊst/
not later than . . . /ˌnɒt 'leɪtə ðæn . . ./
text /tekst/
earthquake /'ɜ:θkweɪk/
suburb /'sʌbɜ:b/

check in (*v.*) /tʃek 'ɪn/
piece /pi:s/
baggage /'bægɪdʒ/
hand baggage /'hænd bægɪdʒ/
label /'leɪbl/
smoking /'sməʊkɪŋ/
non-smoking /'nɒnsməʊkɪŋ/
window seat /'wɪndəʊ si:t/
aisle /aɪl/
boarding card /'bɔ:dɪŋ kɑ:d/
departure gate /dɪ'pɑ:tʃə geɪt/

cancel /'kænsl/
overweight /ˌəʊvə'weɪt/
valid /'vælɪd/
visa /'vi:zə/
section /'sekʃn/

fine /faɪn/
ready /'redɪ/
taxi /'tæksɪ/
pilot /'paɪlət/

spaceship /'speɪsʃɪp/

UNIT 10 PROBLEMS

upset (*adj.*) /ʌp'set/
cause /kɔ:z/
treat /tri:t/
allowed /ə'laʊd/
fair /feə(r)/
leave . . . alone /ˌli:v . . . ə'ləʊn/
get over . . . /ˌget əʊvə(r) '. . ./
sensible /'sensəbl/
fed up with . . . /ˌfed 'ʌp wɪð . . ./
dye /daɪ/
What on earth . . . ? /ˌwɒt ɒn 'ɜ:θ . . ./
never mind /ˌnevə 'maɪnd/
empty /'emptɪ/
gone /gɒn/

resolution /ˌrezə'lu:ʃn/
alcohol /'ælkəhɒl/
university /ˌu:nɪ'vɜ:sətɪ/
slot machine /'slɒt məʃi:n/
bank loan /'bæŋk ləʊn/
crime /kraɪm/
channel /'tʃænl/
malaria /mə'leərɪə/
confession /kən'feʃn/
cannibal /'kænɪbl/

advice /əd'vaɪs/
spots /spɒts/

acne /'æknɪ/
laugh /lɑ:f/
medicated /'medɪkeɪtɪd/
fresh /freʃ/
vegetable /'vedʒtəbl/
worrying /'wʌrɪɪŋ/
guilty /'gɪltɪ/
invite /ɪn'vaɪt/
give up /gɪv 'ʌp/
a couple of weeks ago /ə ˌkʌpl əv 'wi:ks əgəʊ/
midnight /'mɪdnaɪt/
bullying /'bʊlɪɪŋ/
gang /gæŋ/
hell /hel/
push /pʊʃ/
hit /hɪt/
fool /fu:l/
bus fare /'bʌs feə(r)/
purse /pɜ:s/
face /feɪs/
frightened /'fraɪtənd/
surprised /sə'praɪzd/
mess /mes/
unattractive /ˌʌnə'træktɪv/
worse /wɜ:s/

Quebec /kwɪ'bek/
wrap /ræp/
untie /ʌn'taɪ/
knot /nɒt/
absolute /'æbsəlu:t/
wreck /rek/
Gaul /gɔ:l/
fancy dress /ˌfænsɪ 'dres/

---

lucky /'lʌkɪ/
wash /wɒʃ/
chicken /'tʃɪkən/
feed /fi:d/
seem /si:m/
afford /ə'fɔ:d/
indoors /ɪn'dɔ:z/
play /pleɪ/
worry about . . . /ˌwʌrɪ əbaʊt '. . ./
work hard /ˌwɜ:k 'hɑ:d/
simple /'sɪmpl/

---

proverb /'prɒvɜ:b/
glitter /'glɪtə(r)/
hatch /hætʃ/
silver /'sɪlvə(r)/
lining /'laɪnɪŋ/

UNIT 11 THE TRUTH

leave home /li:v 'həʊm/
run away /ˌrʌn ə'weɪ/
together /tə'geðə(r)/
silly /'sɪlɪ/
schoolgirl /'sku:lgɜ:l/
because of . . . /bɪˌkɒz əv '. . ./
at the door /ət ðə 'dɔ:(r)/
fiancee /fɪ'ɒnseɪ/
unfriendly /ʌn'frendlɪ/
put two and two together /pʊt ˌtu: ən ˌtu: tə'geðə(r)/
such a fool /ˌsʌtʃ ə 'fu:l/

---

secretary /'sekrətrɪ/
the boss /ðə 'bɒs/
care for . . . /ˌkeə fɔ:(r) '. . ./

---

two-litre /tu: li:tə(r)/
sunroof /'sʌnru:f/
leather /'leðə(r)/
seat /si:t/
decide /dɪ'saɪd/
safari park /sə'fɑ:rɪ pɑ:k/
wreck /rek/
damage /'dæmɪdʒ/
smell /smel/
brandy /'brændɪ/
breathalyser /'breθəlaɪzə(r)/
positive /'pɒsətɪv/
mother-in-law /'mʌðərɪnlɔ:/
tired /'taɪəd/
message /'mesɪdʒ/
loudspeaker /ˌlaʊd'spi:kə(r)/
horrified /'hɒrəfaɪd/
aerial /'eərɪəl/
trunk /trʌŋk/
remember /rɪ'membə(r)/
warden /'wɔ:dn/
trumpet /'trʌmpɪt/
trap /træp/
faint /feɪnt/
fetch /fetʃ/
hammer /'hæmə(r)/
set free /set 'fri:/
wheel /wi:l/
windscreen wiper /'wɪndskri:n waɪpə(r)/
owner /'əʊnə(r)/
the news /ðə 'nju:z/
a serious accident /ə ˌsɪərɪəs 'æksɪdənt/
the M1 /ðə əm 'wʌn/
thick /θɪk/
fog /fɒg/
injure /'ɪndʒə(r)/
foggy /'fɒgɪ/
weather /'weðə(r)/
assassinate /ə'sæsɪneɪt/
spokesman /'spəʊksmən/
former /'fɔ:mə(r)/
bank robbery /'bæŋk rɒbərɪ/
in the early hours /ˌɪn ðɪ ˌɜ:lɪ 'aʊəz/
fit /fɪt/
match /mætʃ/
broadcasters /'brɔ:dkɑ:stəz/
spokesperson /'spəʊkspɜ:sn/
witness /'wɪtnɪs/

UNIT 12 REVISION

rhinoceros /raɪ'nɒsərəs/
in danger of . . . /ɪn ˌdeɪndʒər əv '. . ./
extinction /ɪk'stɪŋkʃn/
one-horned /'wʌn hɔ:nd/
rarest /'reərɪst/
grass /grɑ:s/
leaf /li:f/
extinct /ɪk'stɪŋkt/
protect /prə'tekt/
short-sighted /ʃɔ:t 'saɪtɪd/
aggressive /ə'gresɪv/
weigh /weɪ/
tonnes /tʌnz/
enemy /'enəmɪ/
horn /hɔ:n/
traditional /trə'dɪʃənl/
as a result /æz ə rɪ'zʌlt/
poacher /'pəʊtʃə(r)/
museum /mju:'zɪəm/
share /ʃeə(r)/
fate /feɪt/

Guess what. /ˌges 'wɒt/
congratulations /kənˌgrætʃʊ'leɪʃnz/
no chance of . . . /nəʊ 'tʃɑ:ns əv . . ./
borrow /'bɒrəʊ/
stupid /'stju:pɪd/
lazy /'leɪzɪ/
selfish /'selfɪʃ/
exhibition /ˌeksɪ'bɪʃn/
good luck /gʊd 'lʌk/
miss /mɪs/

---

declare /dɪ'kleə(r)/
forward /'fɔ:wəd/
marine /mə'ri:n/
threaten /'θretn/
over-fishing /ˌəʊvə 'fɪʃɪŋ/
fund /fʌnd/
flood /flʌd/
dam /dæm/
oil tanker /'ɔɪl tæŋkə(r)/
coastline /'kəʊstlaɪn/
panda /'pændə/
waste /weɪst/
sink /sɪŋk/
drought /draʊt/
starvation /stɑ:'veɪʃn/
whaling /'weɪlɪŋ/
ban /bæn/
rare /reə(r)/
worldwide /ˌwɜ:ld'waɪd/
huge /hju:dʒ/
delta /'deltə/
tiger /'taɪgə(r)/
oil slick /'ɔɪl slɪk/
breeding ground /'bri:dɪŋ graʊnd/
turtle /'tɜ:tl/
tropical /'trɒpɪkl/
dump /dʌmp/
shellfish /'ʃelfɪʃ/

Irregular verbs

Infinitive verbs	Past tense	Past participle
be /bɪ, bi:/	was /wəz, wɒz/	been /bɪn, bi:n/
become /bɪˈkʌm/	became /bɪˈkeɪm/	become /bɪˈkʌm/
blow /bləʊ/	blew /blu:/	blown /bləʊn/
break /breɪk/	broke /brəʊk/	broken /ˈbrəʊkən/
bring /brɪŋ/	brought /brɔ:t/	brought /brɔ:t/
buy /baɪ/	bought /bɔ:t/	bought /bɔ:t/
catch /kætʃ/	caught /kɔ:t/	caught /kɔ:t/
choose /tʃu:z/	chose /tʃəʊz/	chosen /ˈtʃəʊzn/
come /kʌm/	came /keɪm/	come /kʌm/
cost /kɒst/	cost /kɒst/	cost /kɒst/
do /du:/	did /dɪd/	done /dʌn/
drive /draɪv/	drove /drəʊv/	driven /ˈdrɪvn/
eat /i:t/	ate /et/	eaten /ˈi:tn/
fall /fɔ:l/	fell /fel/	fallen /ˈfɔ:lən/
feed /fi:d/	fed /fed/	fed /fed/
fight /faɪt/	fought /fɔ:t/	fought /fɔ:t/
find /faɪnd/	found /faʊnd/	found /faʊnd/
fly /flaɪ/	flew /flu:/	flown /fləʊn/
forget /fəˈget/	forgot /fəˈgɒt/	forgotten /fəˈgɒtn/
get /get/	got /gɒt/	got /gɒt/
give /gɪv/	gave /geɪv/	given /ˈgɪvn/
go /gəʊ/	went /went/	gone /gɒn/
grow /grəʊ/	grew /gru:/	grown /grəʊn/
have /hæv/	had /hæd/	had /hæd/
hear /hɪə(r)/	heard /hɜ:d/	heard /hɜ:d/
hide /haɪd/	hid /hɪd/	hidden /ˈhɪdn/
hit /hɪt/	hit /hɪt/	hit /hɪt/
hold /həʊld/	held /held/	held /held/
leave /li:v/	left /left/	left /left/
lose /lu:z/	lost /lɒst/	lost /lɒst/
make /meɪk/	made /meɪd/	made /meɪd/
mean /mi:n/	meant /ment/	meant /ment/
meet /mi:t/	met /met/	met /met/
pay /peɪ/	paid /peɪd/	paid /peɪd/
put /pʊt/	put /pʊt/	put /pʊt/
read /ri:d/	read /red/	read /red/
ride /raɪd/	rode /rəʊd/	ridden /ˈrɪdn/
ring /rɪŋ/	rang /ræŋ/	rung /rʌŋ/
run /rʌn/	ran /ræn/	run /rʌn/
say /seɪ/	said /sed/	said /sed/
see /si:/	saw /sɔ:(r)/	seen /si:n/
sell /sel/	sold /səʊld/	sold /səʊld/
send /send/	sent /sent/	sent /sent/
set /set/	set /set/	set /set/
shine /ʃaɪn/	shone /ʃɒn/	shone /ʃɒn/
sink /sɪŋk/	sank /sæŋk/	sunk /sʌŋk/
stand /stænd/	stood /stʊd/	stood /stʊd/
steal /sti:l/	stole /stəʊl/	stolen /ˈstəʊlən/
take /teɪk/	took /tʊk/	taken /ˈteɪkən/
think /θɪŋk/	thought /θɔ:t/	thought /θɔ:t/
throw /θrəʊ/	threw /θru:/	thrown /θrəʊn/
wake up /weɪk ʌp/	woke up /wəʊk ʌp/	woken up /wəʊkən ʌp/
win /wɪn/	won /wʌn/	won /wʌn/
write /raɪt/	wrote /rəʊt/	written /ˈrɪtn/

Oxford University Press
Walton Street, Oxford OX2 6DP

Oxford New York Toronto Madrid
Delhi Bombay Calcutta Madras Karachi
Kuala Lumpur Singapore Hong Kong Tokyo
Nairobi Dar es Salaam Cape Town
Melbourne Auckland

and associated companies in
Berlin Ibadan

Oxford and Oxford English are trade marks of Oxford University Press

First published 1992

ISBN 0 19 435489 X
0 19 435552 7 (Spain)

Printed in Spain by Cayfosa Industria Grafica

Acknowledgements

The author would like to thank Suzanna, Harsányi (Editorial Manager) and Elana Katz (Editor, freelance) for their tireless efforts in turning manuscript into published work. Thanks are also due to all the people at Oxford University Press who have contributed their skills and ideas to producing this book. Thanks are due in particular to Pearl Bevan (Senior Design Project Manager), Amanda Goodridge (Designer), Penny Mishcon (Art Editor), Sylvia Wheeldon (Editor), Fran Holdsworth (Freelance Designer), Keith Shaw (Freelance Designer), and Malcolm Price (Production).

The author would especially like to record his gratitude to his wife Pamela and his children, without whose support and patience *Hotline* would not have been possible.

The publishers would like to thank all of the ELT teachers and advisors around the world who have given generously of their time to talk about their needs and to comment on the manuscript and sample units of *Hotline*. Our thanks are especially due to:

Silvia Ronchetti (Instituto Superior del Profesorado en Lenguas Vivas, Buenos Aires) in Argentina. Freddy Désir (Inspection de l'Enseignement Secondaire de l'Etat, Brussels), Norbert Jacquinet (Institut Notre-Dame, Brussels) in Belgium. Edit Nagy (National Institute of Education, Budapest), Lyane Szentirmay (Madách Imre Gimnázium, Budapest), Judit Sióréti (Városmajori Gimnázium, Budapest), Ilona Jobbágy (Könyves Kálmán Gimnázium, Budapest) in Hungary. Orazio Marchi (Progetto Speciale Lingue Straniere, Forlì) in Italy. Diana England and Monica Green (International House, Lisbon) in Portugal. Patsy Fuller (Freelance Teacher), Luis Fernandez (I.B. Alexandre Satorras, Mataro), Vincenc Haro and Merce Fosch (I.B. Ferran Casablanca, Sabadell), Eleanor Tompkins (La Salle Congres, Barcelona), Ana Coll (I.B. Narcis Monturiol, Barcelona), Victoria Alcalde (I.B. San Isidro, Madrid), Joaquin Rojo (I.B. Francisco de Goya, Madrid), Pedro Horillo and Margarita Hernandez (I.B. Verdaguer Parc de la Ciutadella, Barcelona), Pilar Gomez (Instituto Cid Campeador, Valencia) in Spain. Carroll Klein (Koç Özel Lisesi, Istanbul) in Turkey.

Special thanks are due to a panel of British teenagers, Juliet Kinsman, Zuleika Melluish, Pema Radha, Alex Huskinson and Mark Killingley, who advised on the Victoria Road storyline and on the Reading and Listening topics and to whom we are indebted for the natural, colloquial teenage language of the Victoria Road characters.

Illustrations by:

Julia Bigg, Anna Brookes, Terry Cripps, Sally Davies, Suzanna English, Alison Everitt, Clive Goodyer, Beverly Levy, Frances Lloyd, Mike Nicholson, Carole Roberts, Judy Stevens, Martin Ursell.

Location photography by: Emily Andersen, Rob Judges.

Victoria Road photography by: John Walmsley.

Studio photography by: Lark Gilmer, Mark Mason.

The characters in Victoria Road were played by:

Jo Craydon, Justine Crossingham, Joseph Derrett, Andrew Doughty, Rowena Doughty, Mari Carmen Ferez, Ron Field, Duncan Hamilton Irving, Emma Harding, Jason Hopperton, Natalie Kowlessur, Robert Paige, Richard Ridgewell, Julia Robson, Ben, Paul, Pat and Sarah Rose, Helen Scott, Patrick Short, Stewart Spelling, Misty the dog.

The publishers and author would like to thank the following for their help with the Victoria Road photo story:

Banstead Sports Centre, British Rail, Kay Dudeney, Robin Emery, Epsom and Ewell Borough Council, Epsom and Ewell High School, Mrs Moretta, Frances Myers, NESCOT Drama Department, Savill and Holdsworth, St Andrew's School (Leatherhead), St Anthony's Hospital, Surrey Ambulance Service, Therfield School (Leatherhead), Thorndyke Youth Theatre, Rose and Brian Walsh, Peel South East.

The publishers and author would like to thank the following for their permission to reproduce photographs:

Allsport Ltd, Ancient Art and Architecture Collection, The Aviation Picture Library, Bridgeman Art Library Ltd, J Allan Cash Ltd, Colorific, Bruce Coleman Ltd, Sylvia Cordaiy, Department of Medical Illustration (St Bartholomew's Hospital), Mary Evans Picture Library, Granada Television, Grundy TV/Aquarius, Robert Harding Picture Library, Michael Holford Picture Library, The Hulton Picture Company, The Image Bank, Impact Photos Ltd, I.T.N. Press Office, London Features International Ltd, Magnum, Peugeot, Popperfoto, Retna Pictures Ltd, Sygma Ltd, Survival International.

'And Then He Kissed Me' used by kind permission of Carlin Music Corporation Ltd.

The publishers and author would like to thank the following organizations for their help and co-operation:

Amnesty International, Avondate Park Primary School (London), Body Shop International Plc, Channel 4 News, Chickens Lib, Greenpeace Ltd, Oxfam, Pizza By-Numbers (London), Shelter – National Campaign for The Homeless, Survival International, Wild Oats (London).